Places to Pray

Holy Sites in Catholic Missouri

Patrick Murphy

Copyright © 2023. Reedy Press, LLC
All rights reserved.

Reedy Press
PO Box 5131
St. Louis, MO 63139
www.reedypress.com

No part of this publication may be reproduced or transmitted in any form or
by any means, electronic or mechanical, including photocopy, recording, or
any information storage and retrieval system, without permission in writing
from the publisher.

Permission may be sought directly from Reedy Press at the above mailing
address or via our website at www.reedypress.com.

Library of Congress Control Number: 2022949151

ISBN: 9781681064369

Design by Richard Roden

Cover photo of author, Ursula Ruhl

All images are courtesy of the author or believed to
be in the public domain unless noted otherwise.

Printed in the United States

23 24 25 26 27   5 4 3 2 1

Table of Contents

Archdiocese of St. Louis—Beyond the City

Diocese of Kansas City—St. Joseph

Diocese of Jefferson City

Diocese of Springfield—Cape Girardeau

Acknowledgments

Several people have generously given their time and expertise to make this a better book than I ever could have written without them. Carol Campbell, director of the Old Ferdinand Shrine, steered me from errors in fact and nuance in sections dealing with special pathways to prayer and elements of Catholic culture. Thanks as well to Jay Nies, editor of the *Catholic Missourian*, who guided me in reporting on Catholic communities within the Diocese of Jefferson City.

I'm grateful to all the parish staff, pastors, abbots and abbesses, and religious brothers and sisters throughout the state who welcomed me into their communities. Once again, my friends at Reedy Press, particularly Josh Stevens and Barb Northcott, have worked their usual magic in turning a bunch of words and pictures into a real book. Biggest thanks of all go to my wife, Annie, who loves me enough to give me her honest opinions.

Simon of Cyrene helps Jesus at St. Peter Catholic Church in Kirkwood.

A Word to the Wise

As you plan your pilgrimages to various sites, it's a good idea to visit their websites or give them a call before showing up. Descriptions of all the destinations include contact information. Many churches are locked during certain hours, but someone in the parish office is usually happy to let you in if you call ahead. In some of the tiniest villages, it's not unusual for a neighbor or shopkeeper to take calls from curious visitors and conduct personal tours.

Most churches rely heavily upon donations to remain open. Many are old and require maintenance. It's a constant struggle. Your prayers are always appreciated, but donations are welcome, too, making it possible for these holy sites to serve generations to come.

. . . And a Mea Culpa

The richness of Missouri's Catholic heritage made it impossible to include every holy site worthy of mention. If a place that's special to you isn't included, no slight was intended. Keeping the selection within the limits of a portable volume called for subjective and painful decisions. The objective was to include places of historical or architectural interest and represent a range of races, nationalities, and flavors of Catholicism. In a state where Catholics live in significantly larger numbers in certain areas, some regions got more attention than others.

So, it's not an encyclopedia or comprehensive catalog. It's a sampling of interesting places. And that's why some beautiful, historical, and beloved churches, shrines, chapels, grottos, convents, and monasteries are not included.

I ask for your forgiveness.

A Rich Catholic Heritage

For more than 300 years, Roman Catholics have shaped the history and culture of Missouri. Where they settled and remain to this day is due largely to historical trends going back to the earliest days of European colonialism in the New World.

In 1673, Father Jacques Marquette first paddled along Missouri's riverbanks, opening the way for French exploration. Catholic Spain and France took turns governing, but the larger number of French traders and trappers gave them the upper hand. Towns like St. Charles, Ste. Genevieve, Portage des Sioux, and Florissant had a distinctly French flavor. French Vincentians settled in Perryville, establishing a strong Catholic presence that continues today. In 1823, 20 years after the United States bought the Louisiana territory, the city of St. Louis was still half French and Catholic.

In the early years of the 19th century Anglo-American migration came to overshadow French influence, but by mid-century famine and political oppression brought waves of Catholic immigrants from Ireland, Germany, Italy, and Eastern Europe. Many moved to St. Louis. The hills and rich farmland south of the Missouri River attracted large numbers of Germans, both Protestant and Catholic, who were reminded of their homeland. German Catholic communities are still strong in towns like Washington and Hermann. Catholics settled in central and northern Missouri in smaller numbers in the years following the Civil War, and many small towns near Jefferson City still take pride in their Catholic identities. On the western side of the state, St. Joseph and Kansas City received large numbers of Irish and German immigrants, then Hispanics, Italians, and Asians.

Old World prejudices followed the new arrivals, prompting Catholics and Protestants to live separately. Nativism and the violent, anti-Catholic, Know-Nothing movement in the mid-19th century kept many Catholic immigrants within their ethnic, urban neighborhoods. A group of St. Louis Irish struck out in the 1850s to resettle near the Arkansas border, hoping to escape the dismal conditions of the city. It turned out to be an unhappy venture, as they found themselves caught in the crosshairs of both Union and Confederate troops during the Civil War. Those who survived bloody raids fled to cities in southern Missouri, and today the area is known as the Irish Wilderness.

Missionary and explorer
Fr. Jacques Marquette, SJ.
Missouri Historical Society, St. Louis.

An anti-Catholic weekly newspaper called the *Menace* (later renamed the *Monitor*) was published in central Missouri between 1911 and 1942, stirring up local prejudice. Today, religion in the Ozarks trends toward Pentecostal and Evangelical denominations.

Today the old prejudices have largely disappeared. Catholics from around the world continue to move to Missouri, bringing their own traditions as they find their place in cities and towns across the state. In the spirit of those who came before them, they continue the tradition of building memorials to their faith and places to pray.

HWY 170

RT 367

HWY 70

BADEN
5

RT 115

RT 180

MISSISSIPPI
RIVER

RT 3

COLLEGE HILL
4

HWY 70

MCKINLEY
BRIDGE

3

NORTH GRAND
7

HYDE PARK

CENTRAL WEST END
2

11

HWY 70

16

DOWNTOWN STL

8

GRAND CENTER

20

HWY 64

DOGTOWN
18

1

RT 100

21

HWY 55

12

HWY 44

19 22

THE HILL

FOX PARK

6

15

SOULARD

17

RT 366

10

ST. LOUIS HILLS

HWY 55

RT 30

13

RT 3

DUTCHTOWN

14

HWY 55

9

CARONDELET

HWY 55

RT 231

**SEE CORRESPONDING NUMBERS
ON THE FOLLOWING PAGES.**

Archdiocese
of St. Louis

ST. LOUIS CITY

Basilica of St. Louis, King of France *(The Old Cathedral)*

St. Louis City—Riverfront

209 Walnut St.	314.231.3250	**MAP LOCATION #1**
St. Louis 63102	Oldcathedralstl.org	

There are few buildings in St. Louis more beloved than the old stone church that stands on the grounds of the Gateway Arch. It's survived two centuries of change, including cholera epidemics and a fire in 1849 that destroyed the heart of the city. Parishioners defended it from Nativist mobs before the Civil War and urban developers after World War II.

When Pierre Laclede and Auguste Chouteau founded St. Louis in 1764, they dedicated a plot of land within the village as the site for a Catholic church. Priests celebrated Mass in a tent until a log church was built in 1770, and one of brick in 1818. For years it was the only church of any denomination in St. Louis. The current structure, designed in the Greek Revival style popular at the time, was completed in 1834. In 1961, Pope John XXIII designated it a basilica in the name of the city's namesake, Louis IX of France.

Shrine to Our Lady of Fatima at the Old Cathedral.

In 1970, Cardinal John Carberry made a pilgrimage to Fatima, Portugal, where the Virgin Mary appeared several times in 1917. When he returned, he had a shrine to Our Lady of Fatima placed in the Cathedral, encouraging people to pray for peace in our troubled world.

When you offer a prayer at the Old Cathedral, you share the hope that it may be heard with generations of pioneers, immigrants, and their descendants who have come before you to that same holy place.

Our Lady of Fatima

The statue of Our Lady of Fatima displayed in the Old Cathedral is a replica of the one in Fatima, Portugal, the site of multiple apparitions of the Virgin Mary.

Between May and October of 1917, three shepherd children reported six encounters with the Virgin Mary, whom they described

Holy card,
Our Lady of Fatima.

as "a lady all in white . . . more brilliant than the sun." The children claimed to have experienced a variety of visions and predictions of wars and troubles. They were told to say the Rosary daily and pray for peace. The lady also predicted that there would be a miracle in October for all to see and believe.

Word spread quickly, prompting a flurry among believers and critics alike, and on October 13, more than 70,000 people gathered in anticipation of the predicted miracle. Something did indeed happen that day, which has become known as the Miracle of the Sun.

The crowd gathered around the children who, as they later reported, were seeing a panorama of visions including Jesus, Mary, and Joseph blessing the assembly. It had rained all morning, but suddenly it stopped, and the clouds parted. Then, as many testified afterward, the sun transformed into an opaque, spinning disc, casting multicolored lights in all directions. To the horror of many, it appeared to dance, then hurtle toward earth, stop, and zigzag back to its proper place in the sky. The phenomenon lasted about 10 minutes and was reported as far away as 10 miles.

Among those who affirmed the strange happenings were news reporters, local officials, and even church leaders who had been skeptical of the children's claims. Reports varied: some saw only the colors; others saw nothing out of the ordinary. Photographs taken at the time showed nothing unusual. A variety of rational explanations include mass hypnosis, the power of suggestion, weather patterns, and stratospheric dust clouds.

And there is the explanation that it was a miracle, delivered by the Holy Mother to encourage us to pray for peace.

The shepherd children, from left: Jacinta and Francisco Marto, and Lúcia dos Santos.

Oh my Jesus, I offer this for love of Thee,
for the conversion of sinners, and in
reparation for the sins committed against the
Immaculate Heart of Mary.

The Sacred Prayer Taught to the Shepherd Children
by the Blessed Mother

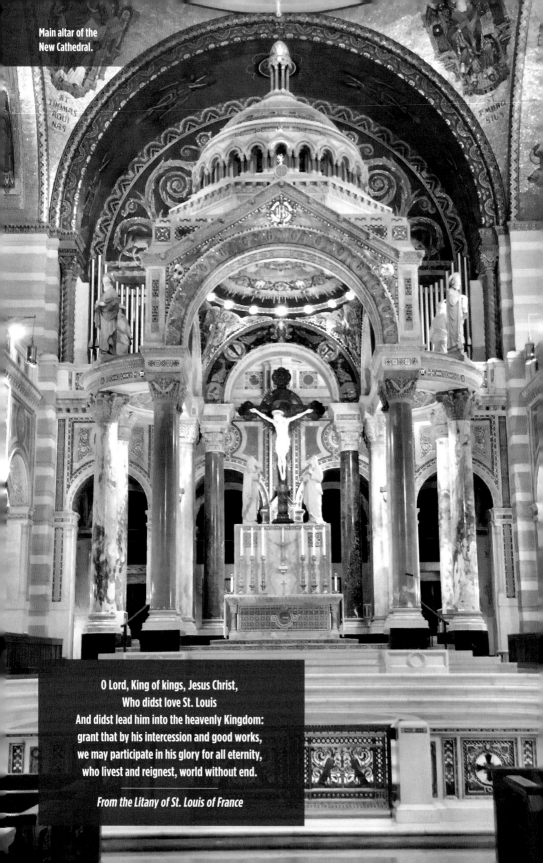

Main altar of the New Cathedral.

O Lord, King of kings, Jesus Christ,
Who didst love St. Louis
And didst lead him into the heavenly Kingdom:
grant that by his intercession and good works,
we may participate in his glory for all eternity,
who livest and reignest, world without end.

From the Litany of St. Louis of France

Cathedral Basilica of St. Louis *(The New Cathedral)*

St. Louis City—Central West End

4431 Lindell Blvd.   314.373.8200   MAP LOCATION #2
St. Louis 63108   Cathedralstl.org

Shrine of the Sacred Heart, created by the Vatican's Mosaic Studio.

It is magnificent. In matters of design and elegance, the Cathedral Basilica of St. Louis holds its own with the great cathedrals of the world. From the street it is massive and medieval. Its interior is dazzling and Byzantine, immersing visitors in centuries of Catholic tradition through art and architecture.

By the turn of the 20th century, decades of European immigration had made St. Louis one of the major Catholic cultural centers in America. The Archdiocese of St. Louis had outgrown its old cathedral by the river, and the city was spreading west. When Archbishop John Glennon dedicated the new cathedral in the city's Central West End in 1914, it was an immediate source of pride for Catholics and non-Catholics alike.

It defies description. Its walls and ceilings are covered with one of the largest installations of mosaics in the world, depicting Christian traditions, scenes from the Gospels, and moments in the lives of the saints. A shrine to the Sacred Heart of Jesus features a mosaic made of 30 varieties of marble and onyx. Its two large rose windows were designed by Tiffany and Company. The Cathedral's collections of stained glass, sculpture, and paintings rival those of many museums.

Visitors tend to fall into two categories: tourists and worshippers. No one can possibly take it all in during a single visit. For those who come to pray, it's worth considering that this lavish space is not intended just to impress, but also to inspire the spirit to a occupy a higher place. There are many quiet spaces here. You might choose to offer your prayers in a side chapel or a place near a piece of art that has meaning for you or brings you peace.

As you seek God in this amazing space, your heart will know that the magnificence of even the greatest cathedral can never be more than an imitation of the infinite grandeur of God.

Most Holy Trinity Catholic Church

St. Louis City—Hyde Park

3519 N 14th St.
St. Louis 63107

314.241.9165
Mhtstl.org

MAP LOCATION #3

The twin spires of Most Holy Trinity are a familiar landmark to the thousands of motorists who travel past north St. Louis every day on Interstate 70, but few are aware of its history. It's the third church to stand on the site since the parish was established in 1848, when it was part of a German village called New Bremen.

The neighborhood still identified as German when the current church opened in 1909. There was never a doubt that it should be a grand building. Inspired by the Cathedral in Strasbourg, France, it was constructed of Indiana limestone, a material often reserved for government buildings. The windows were created in the style of Bavarian stained glass by the German craftsman Emil Frei Sr. One window, commissioned by the parish's young men's sodality, was designed as a "Tribute to America" after World War I to assure the city's non-German neighborhoods of their patriotism.

As churches in the surrounding neighborhoods closed, it opened its doors to their congregants and made room for their liturgical treasures. Today it holds onto its place above the highway in a world its founders could never have imagined. Despite the changes, Most Holy Trinity's dedication to God's Purpose remains constant.

Baptism of Christ, depicted in one of the church's finely crafted windows.

St. Paul keeps watch in the nave of Most Holy Trinity.

O, Omnipotence of the Father,
help my fragility
and save me from the depths of misery.

O, Wisdom of the Son,
direct all my thoughts,
my words, and my deeds.

O, Love of the Holy Spirit,
be the source of all the actions of my mind,
that they may always be conformed
to God's good pleasure.

Adoration by the Pink Sisters continues in their chapel for almost a century without interruption.

Come, Holy Spirit, fill the hearts of your faithful,
and kindle in them the fire of your love.
Send forth your Spirit and they shall be created.
And you will renew the face of the earth.

From Prayer of the Holy Spirit

Mount Grace Convent of the Holy Spirit Adoration Sisters *(Pink Sisters)*

St. Louis City—College Hill

1438 E Warne Ave.	314.381.5686	**MAP LOCATION #4**
St. Louis 63107	Mountgraceconvent.org	

They spend their lives cloistered behind convent walls and grilles, adhering to vows of obedience, chastity, poverty, and silence. They know most people find it hard to understand their small community's way of life, but they insist that they are far from isolated. The Holy Spirit, they say, gives them strength to live disciplined, contemplative lives and open their hearts to the joys and despairs of the world.

Their official name is the Holy Spirit Adoration Sisters, but everyone calls them the Pink Sisters because of their rose-colored habits. The color is a cheerful reminder of God's love. They began their perpetual adoration of the Blessed Sacrament on the first day they moved into their new chapel and convent in June of 1928. Since then, the surrounding neighborhood has fallen into disrepair, but their prayers have continued 24 hours a day, seven days a week, without interruption. Upon entering their Chapel of Perpetual Adoration, you'll always see at least one of the sisters praying behind a screen before the monstrance holding the Blessed Sacrament.

It's surprisingly busy for a place so dedicated to being apart from the world. The chapel is open for daily Mass, personal prayer, Adoration, and Liturgy of the Hours. Petitioners regularly come to the convent requesting prayers for friends and family. Others send in prayer requests through email. A spiritual organization called the Legion of 1000 Adorers guarantees a steady stream of worshippers.

Offering continual and never-ending prayer for the entire world is a formidable task. The Pink Sisters take it on with determination and good cheer. They invite you to join them in this place they've created, which most certainly has the serious attention of the Almighty.

The Pink Sisters occupy a special place in the hearts of many St. Louisans.

Eucharistic Adoration

We've turned our world into such a noisy place, it's easy to think of silence as emptiness or absence. But silence can be the space in which we hear God. It was in silence that Elijah heard God on the mountain, and where St. Thérèse, the Little Flower, found her space to pray. We rarely hold back in expressing our thoughts, to each other and to God. But our fellow mortals are generally not all that interested, and God already knows what we want. So maybe silence is an option worth exploring. That tiny whisper? It might be the Holy Spirit.

Eucharistic Adoration is a chance to try it out. During regular, designated times churches display the consecrated host in a receptacle called a monstrance. For an extended period, the faithful place themselves before it in contemplation and prayer. It's an important practice, since Catholic doctrine confirms that Jesus Christ is present in the host, not just symbolically, but truly, even though the host retains its appearance as bread.

This is not supposed to be easy to understand. It runs counter to most of what we have learned from our senses, practical experience, and the patterns of rational thought that get us through most of our days. But believing something you don't understand is the essence of faith, and faith is a helpful tool for understanding those aspects of the universe that pure reason has not shown itself adequately equipped to explain.

Next time you attend Adoration, you are welcome to spend the time wrestling with your rational mind to make sense of it all. Or you can opt for a sacred silence in which your heart finds the peace it needs to find its own way and maybe even guide you to a place where you may hear the voice of God. He's probably been waiting for a chance to get a word in.

Monstrance with host at
Our Holy Redeemer Catholic Church
in Webster Groves.

O, Jesus, on this day you have fulfilled all my desires.

From now on, near the Eucharist, I shall be able to
sacrifice myself in silence,
to wait for Heaven in peace.

Keeping myself open to the rays of the Divine Host,
in this furnace of love,
I shall be consumed, and like a seraphim,
Lord, I shall love You.

St. Thérèse of Lisieux

Our Lady of the Holy Cross Catholic Church

St. Louis City—Baden

8115 Church Rd.
St. Louis 63147

314.381.0323
Ourladyoftheholycross.org

MAP LOCATION #5

The community of Baden developed as a small trading center around an intersection of farm roads connecting north St. Louis County to the city. In 1857, Archbishop Peter Kenrick bought a nearby farm and turned it into Calvary Cemetery. When Holy Cross was founded in 1863, Baden, as the name suggests, was predominantly German. The current church was built in 1909 and took the name Our Lady of the Holy Cross when it merged with Our Lady of Mount Carmel in the 1990s. Today it serves a diverse congregation in a neighborhood that is mostly African American.

When the new church was constructed, Baden's bustling business district ran for blocks along North Broadway. The neighborhood's former glory has faded, but the church's tall steeple is still visible throughout an area that has the feel of a small town. Holy Cross's large grassy lot gives it space to breathe and show off its impressive, Gothic lines.

The interior has a surprisingly light and airy mood. Unusually tall stained glass windows line the walls, pulling the eyes heavenward. Several carved and painted triptychs portray the lives of the saints, their small doors opening and closing with the seasons. A relic of St. Francis resides in the sanctuary. It is a quiet and peaceful place. Beyond its walls, the world moves on.

The main altar demonstrates the elaborate craftsmanship valued by its original German parishioners.

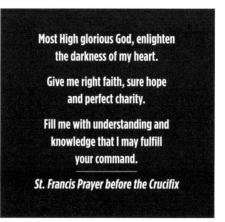

Most High glorious God, enlighten the darkness of my heart.

Give me right faith, sure hope and perfect charity.

Fill me with understanding and knowledge that I may fulfill your command.

St. Francis Prayer before the Crucifix

With pews clustered around the sanctuary, the interior is spacious and open.

Saints Peter and Paul Catholic Church

St. Louis City—Soulard

1919 S 7th St.
St. Louis 63104

314.231.9923
Stspeterandpaulstl.org

MAP LOCATION #6

When the congregants of Saints Peter and Paul laid the cornerstone for their church in 1874, they left no doubt as to its German heritage. The architect was a graduate of the Royal Academy of Architecture in Berlin; the style was German Gothic. In 1890, they added a towering spire as an afterthought, ensuring that their church would not be lost among the crowded streets of the Soulard neighborhood.

As in the case of many urban, ethnic churches, industrialization and postwar exodus reduced the congregation to the point where it was barely able to support such a large church. The neighborhood got a boost in the 1980s when a wave of urban pioneers moved in, attracted by antebellum architecture and low prices. The church adapted, rearranging its interior to create a more intimate configuration. The rows of old pews were taken out, replaced by tiers of benches around the altar. The nave is open and spacious with room to walk about and admire the original 19th-century ornamentation.

Today the neighborhood is largely gentrified, though not all its residents have benefited from the newfound prosperity. For them the church operates a shelter, distributes meals, provides clothing, and offers a range of other social services. But how could a church named after Christianity's most beloved saintly duo do anything less than provide for its neighbors?

Five altars grace the interior.

Saints Teresa and Bridget Catholic Church

St. Louis City—North Grand

2401 N Grand Blvd.   314.371.1190   **MAP LOCATION #7**
St. Louis 63106   Ststb.org

With its large yard facing Grand Boulevard, a splendid stone façade, and two octagonal towers, there's something of the palatial to Saints Teresa and Bridget. Originally dedicated in 1900 as St. Teresa of Avila, it took on a sister saint when the traditional Irish parish of St. Bridget of Erin closed. Today its congregation is predominantly African American and well-known for its programs providing services to the surrounding community.

Saints Teresa and Bridget is often called the Sistine Chapel of north St. Louis because of the large tapestries on its ceiling depicting scenes from Scripture. Other works of art include its high altar, decorated with a mosaic of Christ in the role of a priest, blessing the host.

It's a church worthy to be named after two remarkable women, spiritual powerhouses, whose lives, separated by a thousand years, are still revered by the Church they served.

What Is a Shrine?

Shrines aren't exclusively Roman Catholic; many religions have them in one form or another. Generally, a shrine is a place where people go to contemplate the Divine. Typically, they display, in quiet and meditative spaces, holy objects, or artistic representations—statues, paintings, mosaics—of sacred events or holy people.

Among Christians, some Protestant denominations have shrines, but most are Catholic. Some sites become shrines when local church officials pronounce them as such. National shrines are approved by the US Council of Bishops after meeting strict requirements tying them to traditions and mysteries of the Church. Some have no official status at all but are nevertheless revered by a local community of believers. Shrines can be small spaces in a convent garden, a cemetery, or beside a road. Others are large and more elaborate. They often take the form of a small altar or alcove inside a church. Most include a statue or image of Christ, the Virgin Mary, or a partic-ular saint. They're frequently bathed in soft light from a stained glass window. Small gifts or notes are sometimes left in gratitude for answered prayers.

Grounds of the National Shrine of Our Lady of the Miraculous Medal in Perryville.

Catholics speak affectionately of the "smells and bells" of ritual that facilitate worship. For centuries, the Catholic Church has under-stood the power of art and space to appeal to the senses and raise us beyond the noise of the world. Shrines are not "magical" places. They simply free us from the common distractions of our daily lives and direct our focus toward the infinite and the eternal.

"Be still and know that I am God."

Psalm 46

The Altar of Answered Prayers has graced the Shrine of St. Joseph since 1867.

Hail, Guardian of the Redeemer, Spouse of the Blessed Virgin Mary. To you God entrusted his only Son; in you Mary placed her trust; with you Christ became man.

Blessed Joseph, to us too, show yourself a father and guide us in the path of life. Obtain for us grace, mercy, and courage, and defend us from every evil.

Pope Francis

Shrine of St. Joseph

St. Louis City—Columbus Square

1220 N 11th St.   314.231.9407
St. Louis 63106   Shrineofstjoseph.org

Since its founding in 1843, St. Joseph Church has been celebrated as a place where prayers are answered. Two particularly amazing events established its reputation as the site of a miracle and a shrine to its patron saint.

In 1864, parishioner Ignatius Strecker was severely injured in an industrial accident. His doctor offered no hope for his survival. This occurred while a visiting priest had been invited to preach about the Blessed Peter Claver, known for his intercessory powers with God. Strecker's wife was so impressed that she dragged Ignatius to the church, where he kissed a relic of Claver and was immediately healed. In 1887, the Vatican certified his recovery as a miracle.

That would be impressive enough for most churches, but in 1866, a cholera epidemic set the stage for yet another miraculous occasion. As the death toll that summer rose to 300 a day, a large portion of the parish signed a vow to God, pledging that if their church were spared through the intercession of St. Joseph, they would build a monument in his honor. As it was reported, not a single family member of anyone who signed the pledge died of cholera. The following year the parish installed the magnificent Altar of Answered Prayers, which stands today as testament to their faith.

Known as the Church of Miracles, St. Joseph thrived until the mid-20th century, when urban flight and the destruction of the surrounding neighborhoods reduced it to a dilapidated eyesore. There was talk of demolishing it in the early 1980s, when a friends group accomplished what might be described as yet another miracle, raising money and painstakingly restoring it to its late-19th-century glory.

Visitors to the Shrine of St. Joseph are welcome to pray and meditate amid the beauty and serenity of a place where it seems all things are possible through faith.

Sisters of St. Joseph of Carondelet

St. Louis City—Carondelet

6400 Minnesota Ave.	314.481.8800	**MAP LOCATION #9**
St. Louis 63111	Csjsl.org	

It seems as if there was never a time when the collection of red brick buildings didn't occupy the top of the hill overlooking the Mississippi. The stone wall that surrounds it appears as ancient as the river itself. There is something old, majestic, and permanent about it, as if the hill's only purpose has always been to support the motherhouse of the Sisters of St. Joseph.

When the sisters moved there from France in 1836, Carondelet was a small French village a few miles south of St. Louis. The archdiocese brought them over to establish a school for the deaf and an orphanage. They've been living and working on the same site ever since, though their mission has expanded over the years to include a variety of social services. In 1841, they built the convent, which is today a city landmark. In 1899, they dedicated the Holy Family Chapel, which still rises above the rooftops of its 19th-century, working-class neighborhood.

The chapel, open to visitors of all faiths, is a bright and open space. Despite its size, it offers a sense of comfort and intimacy. Side chapels preserve treasures from the Sisters' long history, including relics of martyrs from the days of Roman persecution.

Upon entering the chapel, guests pass a marble font of holy water set upon a granite base. Inscribed in gold, in both English and French, are the words, "That All May be One."

O Saint Joseph, do assist me by your powerful intercession,
and obtain for me from your Divine Son
all spiritual blessings, through Jesus Christ, our Lord,
So that, having engaged here below your heavenly power,
I may offer my thanksgiving and homage to the most Loving of Fathers.

From Novena to St. Joseph

The Sisters of St. Joseph's Martyrs Chapel, carved in 1880, houses relics from the earliest days of Christianity.

At the center of St. Agatha's altar is the Image of Divine Mercy, which first appeared in a vision to a Polish nun.

St. Agatha Polish Roman Catholic Church

St. Louis City—Soulard

3239 S 9th St.
St. Louis 63118

314.772.1603
Polishchurchstlouis.org

MAP LOCATION #10

Catholicism in St. Louis has always been characterized by the variety of its ethnic flavors. During his reign as archbishop from 1847 to his death in 1895, Peter Kenrick of Dublin did his best to ensure that each ethnic group would have its own church. In 1885, the cornerstone was blessed for St. Agatha, one of many German Catholic churches on the city's South Side.

Today it's St. Louis's designated Polish language church. That role belonged to St. Stanislaus Kostka on the North Side until a dispute with the archdiocese resulted in the transfer of the Polish language apostolate to St. Agatha in 2005. Today, Masses and sacraments are held in both Polish and English.

It's a beautiful church, built of red brick with terra cotta and stone decorative accents on its Gothic exterior. Despite the shift in national identity, it's changed little over the past century, and the tradition of St. Louis churches connecting the city with the Old World continues today.

Symbols of Polish pride: a portrait of Karol Józef Wojtyła, Pope Paul II, and a banner proclaiming, in Polish, "Mary, Queen of Poland, Pray for us."

St. Alphonsus Liguori Catholic Church *(Rock Church)*

St. Louis City—Grand Center

1118 N Grand Blvd.
St. Louis 63106

314.533.0304
Stalphonsusrock.org

MAP LOCATION #11

When St. Alphonsus Liguori Church was completed in 1872, Grand Boulevard passed through a mostly undeveloped part of north St. Louis. The massive limestone structure dominated the neighborhood taking shape around it, and it became known as the "Rock."

It took its name after the 18th-century Italian artist, philosopher, priest, and saint, who in 1732 founded the Congregation of the Most Holy Redeemer, commonly known as the Redemptorists. They came to St. Louis in the 1860s to carry out their mission of serving the poor, and 150 years after building the Rock Church, they continue to run programs addressing the needs of the underserved.

St. Alphonsus Church is an interesting mix of cultures, where a predominantly African American congregation celebrates its faith in a German Gothic church. The liturgy reflects the energy and dynamism of African American culture, while a novena is prayed weekly to the

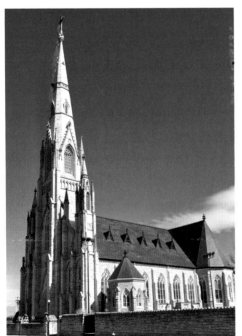

15th-century icon of Our Lady of Perpetual Help.

The Redemptorist order is the protector of the icon, one of the most recognized pieces of Catholic art in the world and a long-standing source of comfort and hope. True to that spirit, the Alphonsus Liguori Rock Church serves as a spiritual and physical haven for the North Grand neighborhood.

The Gothic "Rock" church towers above its neighborhood on St. Louis's Near North Side.

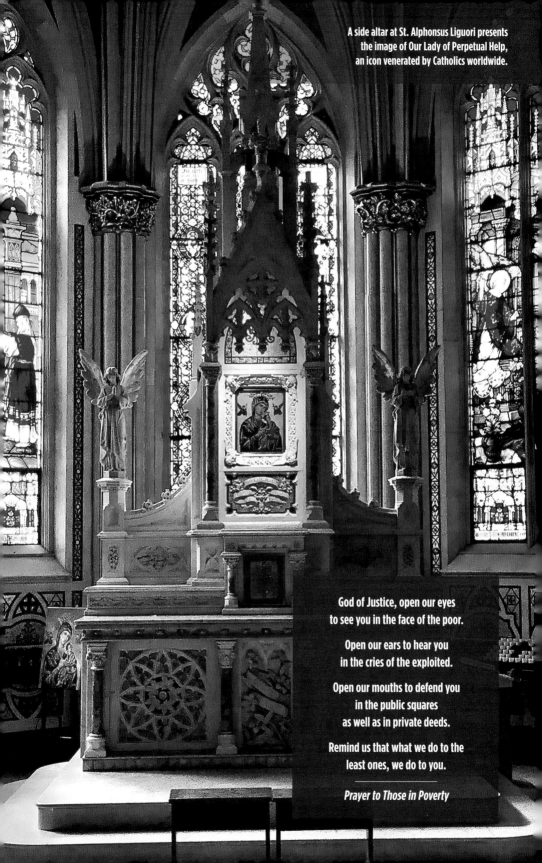

A side altar at St. Alphonsus Liguori presents the image of Our Lady of Perpetual Help, an icon venerated by Catholics worldwide.

God of Justice, open our eyes
to see you in the face of the poor.

Open our ears to hear you
in the cries of the exploited.

Open our mouths to defend you
in the public squares
as well as in private deeds.

Remind us that what we do to the
least ones, we do to you.

Prayer to Those in Poverty

Our Lady of Perpetual Help

The Holy Mother holds her infant son while the Archangels Michael and Gabriel hover nearby, holding the grim tools of Jesus's crucifixion. The icon's history is murky. An artist on the Greek island of Crete created it at least 600 years ago. Today it's one of the world's most recognized and venerated pieces of religious art.

Its migration over the centuries to its current resting place at the Saint Alphonsus of Liguori Church in Rome is a tale of theft, war, coincidences, apparitions, and miracles worthy of a Hollywood production. The short version is that the Holy Mother had some definite opinions about where her icon should hang and, not without drama, successfully communicated her wishes to several of her mortal followers. Some earthly credit goes to the Redemptorist order, which was appointed by the Pope in 1866 as its permanent steward and advocate. When the Redemptorists brought their work to America, devotion to the image spread quickly, particularly among immigrant Catholics. It's not magical, but it certainly is wondrous that an artist could be so inspired to create an image with the power to touch hearts so many years later.

The Virgin Mary's eyes are sorrowful. Jesus clutches her hand and looks anxiously over his shoulder as the Archangels foreshadow his sacrifice. She meets our gaze, sharing her sadness and inviting us to be a part of their story. We do so gladly because we know that at the heart of that story is hope.

Our Lady (also called Our Mother) of Perpetual Help.

Oh Mother of Perpetual Help,
grant that I may ever invoke your perfect name,
the protection of the living and the salvation of the dying.

Purest Mary, let your name henceforth be ever on my lips.

Delay not, Blessed Lady, to rescue me whenever I call on you.

In my temptations, in my needs, I will never cease
to call on you, ever repeating your sacred name, Mary, Mary.

From Novena to Our Mother of Perpetual Help

St. Ambrose Catholic Church

St. Louis City—The Hill

5130 Wilson Ave.   314.771.1228   **MAP LOCATION #12**
St. Louis 63110   Stambroseonthehill.com

Among St. Louis neighborhoods, none embraces its immigrant traditions more closely than the Hill. The first Italians came to St. Louis in the mid-19th century to work on the railroads and in the nearby quarries. For generations, St. Ambrose Church has been the neighborhood's cultural connection to Italy and the unifying force that's carried it through years of social change and shifting populations.

The current St. Ambrose was built in 1926 and, with its Lombard Romanesque architecture, occupies its place in the heart of the Hill as if it were transported there from Italy. Across the street, neighbors gather in a small plaza. The shops, grocery stores, and Italian restaurants are busy. The fire hydrants sport the colors of the Italian flag.

On the feast of Corpus Christi, a large procession carries the Blessed Sacrament through the neighborhood. Every fall the parish holds LaFesta, a celebration of Italian food, music, and culture, attracting visitors from the entire region.

The interior has a comfortable feeling of being much-used and well-loved. The stained glass windows bear the names of families still active in the parish. The walls are adorned with holy objects brought over from Italy and memorials to the parish's historic role as St. Louis's Italian Catholic church. A trinity of faith, tradition, and identity give strength to the church and its community.

The Immigrants, sculpted by Rudoph Torrini, near the entrance to St. Ambrose.

Baptismal font at St. Ambrose.

Oh, Lord, who has mercy upon all,
take away from me my sins,
and mercifully kindle in me the fire
of Your Holy Spirit.
Take away from me the heart of stone,
and give me a heart of flesh,
a heart to love and adore You,
a heart to delight in You,
to follow and enjoy You, for Christ's sake.

St. Ambrose of Milan

The interior of St. Anthony of Padua features decorative work by St. Louis's finest liturgical artisans.

"Go, rebuild my house."

Words heard in prayer by St. Francis of Assisi

St. Anthony of Padua Catholic Church

St. Louis City—Dutchtown

3140 Meramec St.　　　　314.353.7470　　　　**MAP LOCATION #13**
St. Louis 63118　　　　　Stanthonyofpaduastl.com

So great was the influx of German immigrants to St. Louis that one South Side neighborhood took the name of Dutchtown, incorporating a sloppy pronunciation of *Deutsch*. In 1863, the Franciscan Friars of the Sacred Heart Province built a church there to accommodate German-speaking Catholics. They named it after their beloved friar, St. Anthony of Padua. The neighborhood grew rapidly, and in 1910, they built a new church. It was intended to be nothing less than an architectural masterpiece.

It's exquisite and massive, the epitome of German craftsmanship. Designed by a Franciscan brother in the style of Romanesque churches of the Rhineland, it exudes ecclesiastical gravity. Constructed on one of the highest points of the city, its two 175-foot towers are visible from all over South City.

St. Anthony's windows, crafted by German master Emil Frei, take the art of stained glass to new heights, filtering soft light through rich colors, depicting scenes from Scripture. Along the walls, the lives of the saints appear in painted murals.

In 1994, a catastrophic fire damaged much of the church. Under the leadership of the Franciscan Brothers and through the love and hard work of its admirers, the church was restored to its original grandeur.

Risen Christ stands before the Altar to the Sacred Heart of Jesus.

St. Cecilia Catholic Church

St. Louis City—Dutchtown

5418 Louisiana Ave. St. Louis 63111	314.351.1318 Stceciliaparishstl.org	**MAP LOCATION #14**

If you ever have the good luck to attend a St. Cecilia fish fry, you'll regret that Lent lasts only 40 days. The church is famous for bringing Hispanic cuisine to the season of repentance in the best possible way. St. Cecilia began as a German and Irish parish, but today it's one of just a few Catholic churches serving the city's Spanish-speaking population.

Architect Henry P. Hess designed the church, which was dedicated in 1927. Hess also created Rosati-Kain High School, Kenrick-Glennon Seminary, All Saints Catholic Church in University City, and the former Christian Brothers College High School on Clayton Road. The style might be described as sturdy Romanesque with a touch of Gothic to spice it up.

The sanctuary is adorned with Byzantine-style mosaics created by the same group of German artisans who worked on those in the New Cathedral. Light reflects from the thousands of tiny pieces of tile and glass, and above the altar the martyred St. Cecilia makes music with a pair of angels. At times the golden patterns on the wall generate a soft, heavenly glow from the sanctuary. The church's stained glass windows are among the finest in St. Louis's Catholic churches. Many of the statues were carved in Europe, and the marble communion rail and the baldachin above the altar are exquisite works of art.

St. Cecilia is a delight to the senses, from the quality of light that fills it to the many finely crafted objects that adorn it. In the tradition of European cathedrals, it employs art in ways that elevate our spirits and assist us in our journeys of faith.

Side altar to Our Lady of Perpetual Help.

St. Cecilia's display of mosaics is second in size only to that of the New Cathedral.

O glorious saint,
who chose to die
Instead of denying your King,
We pray you please
to help us as
His fair praise we sing!

We lift our hearts in joyous song
to honor Him this way,
And while we sing, remember-
ing, to sing is to doubly pray.

*Prayer to St. Cecilia,
patron saint of music*

The high altar of St. Francis de Sales directs the eyes toward Heaven.

St. Francis de Sales Oratory

St. Louis City—Fox Park

2653 Ohio Ave.
St. Louis 63118

314.771.3100
Institute-christ-king.org/stlouis-home

MAP LOCATION #15

Its local nickname is the "Cathedral of south St. Louis," though it's not officially a cathedral. It certainly looks like one. The architecture is German Gothic, a 19th-century twist on a 13th-century style. The front portal is modeled after the Cathedral of Munich. Its 300-foot steeple makes it one of the tallest buildings in St. Louis and a signature of South City's skyline. The windows were created by German stained glass craftsman Emil Frei Sr. Its interior walls are graced with the murals of another German master, Fridolin Fuchs.

St. Francis de Sales thrived as a center of German American Catholicism until urban flight took most of its parishioners to the suburbs. In 2005, it was slated for demolition, but the archdiocese saved it by turning it into an Oratory and handing its operation over to the Institute of Christ the King Sovereign Priest.

> Do not look forward in fear
> to the changes in life;
> rather, look to them with full hope
> that as they arise,
> God, whose very own you are,
> will lead you safely through all things,
> and when you cannot stand it,
> God will carry you in His arms.
>
> Do not fear what may happen tomorrow;
> the same understanding Father
> who cares for you today
> will take care of you then
> and every day.
>
> He will either shield you from suffering
> or will give you unfailing strength to bear it.
> Be at peace and put aside all
> anxious thoughts and imaginations.
>
> *St. Francis de Sales*

An Oratory is a church which, unlike a parish, does not serve specific boundaries. Under the Institute's guidance, traditional practices of pre-Vatican II Catholicism are encouraged, including the wearing of chapel veils by female parishioners and celebration of the Latin Mass. The church is well-known for its excellent music programs and choirs specializing in Gregorian chants and polyphony.

Many older visitors will be reminded of the Church of their youth. Those growing up since the 1960s can experience some of the sights and sounds of a Catholic church in the days before they were born.

St. Francis Xavier College Church

St. Louis City—Grand Center

3628 Lindell Blvd. 314.977.7300   **MAP LOCATION #16**
St. Louis 63108   Sfxstl.org

The College Church holds a special place in the hearts of St. Louisans. Located on Grand Boulevard in Midtown between the riverfront and the Central West End, it stands securely in the center of the city's cultural geography. In Hollywood's heyday, Grand was the city's "Great, White Way," its blocks lined with glittering movie palaces. When mid-century decline brought poverty and crime to the neighborhood, the church and university were the only remaining anchors. Without them Midtown could never have turned itself around to become the vibrant "Grand Center Arts District" it is today.

The story begins long before construction of the current church. In the 1830s, Saint Louis University established a downtown parish to serve its faculty, staff, and a growing Irish population. Named after the cofounder of the Society of Jesus, St. Xavier's was the first English-speaking parish in a town of French and German neighborhoods.

St. Louis rapidly expanded after the Civil War, and the university relocated its campus to the present site. In 1898, it opened its new church, modeled after St. Colman's Cathedral in Cobh, Ireland. A bell tower was added in 1914. The craftsmen of Emil Frei's studio created the stained glass windows in the 1930s.

College Church is a St. Louis landmark, a gem of Gothic architecture, and one of the Catholic community's top choices for weddings. Today the neighborhood it helped rejuvenate is busy, its sidewalks crowded with young people, artists, academics, and religious. True to its Jesuit heritage, the parish plays an active role in local affairs, hosting ecumenical gatherings and weighing in on issues of social justice. Attracting worshippers from across the metropolitan region, it serves as a bridge between generations, a point of connection among St. Louis's many diverse neighborhoods, and an affirmation of the city's Catholic past and present.

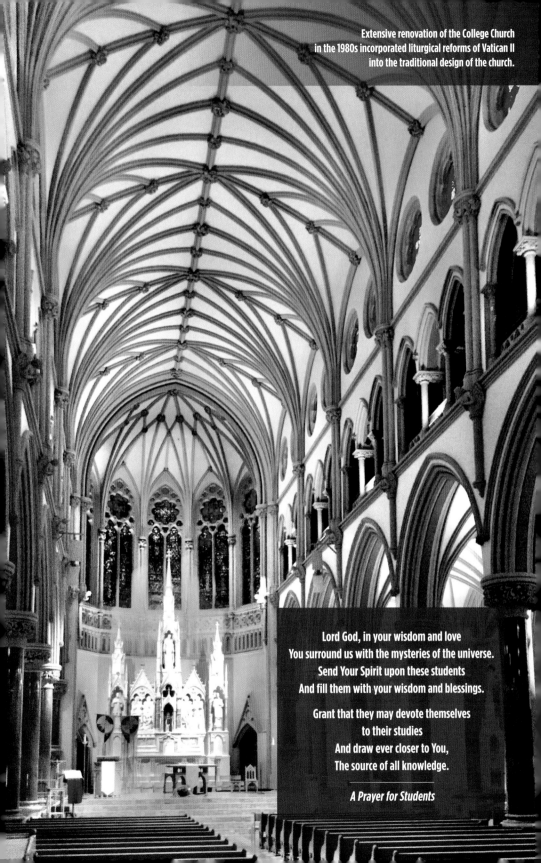

Extensive renovation of the College Church in the 1980s incorporated liturgical reforms of Vatican II into the traditional design of the church.

Lord God, in your wisdom and love
You surround us with the mysteries of the universe.
Send Your Spirit upon these students
And fill them with your wisdom and blessings.

Grant that they may devote themselves
to their studies
And draw ever closer to You,
The source of all knowledge.

A Prayer for Students

St. Gabriel the Archangel Catholic Church

St. Louis City—St. Louis Hills

6303 Nottingham Ave.   314.353.6303   **MAP LOCATION #17**
St. Louis 63109   Stgabrielstl.org

When the parishioners of St. Gabriel decided to build a new church, they created a place of worship unlike any other in the city, a mixture of contemporary and traditional styles capturing a Gothic spirit within a modern design.

In 1950, when St. Gabriel was built, Art Deco had already made way for more minimalist mid-century styles. St. Gabe, as it's affectionately called, is deco imagining itself to be medieval. Its angular exterior of bright limestone is smooth without unnecessary decoration. Its 12-story steeple towers over one of St. Louis's newer neighborhoods, a 1930s mix of Tudor-style apartment buildings and houses modeled after English cottages. True to its deco roots, the steeple has setbacks, creating a marriage of Gothic cathedral and city skyscraper.

The interior has an open feel. There are no supporting columns to obstruct sight lines from the pews, which are arranged in a fan shape. Though the style is unmistakably modern, the church has all the usual trappings, statues, symbols, and artwork of a traditional Roman Catholic Church. Most of the windows are the creations of Emil Frei Jr., son of the original stained glass master, and his colleague Milton Frenzel.

St. Louis artist Siegfried Reinhardt designed the clerestory windows, which portray an angelic choir.

St. Gabriel is one of our busier Archangels, delivering important messages throughout both the Old and New Testaments. His church in St. Louis Hills delivers its own message—that modern and traditional fit well together when they're both telling the same story.

Gothic meets Art Deco.

St. James the Greater Catholic Church

St. Louis City—Dogtown

6401 Wade Ave.   **MAP LOCATION #18**
314.645.0167
St. Louis 63139
Stjamesthegreater.org

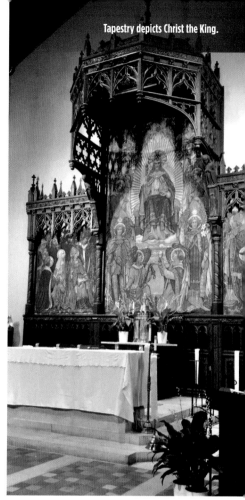

Tapestry depicts Christ the King.

The days of St. Louis's great Irish churches have passed. St. Patrick's, St. Lawrence O'Toole, St. Bridget of Erin, and St. Columbkille have all fallen to the wrecking ball, leaving St. James the Greater in the solitary role of the city's only remaining "Irish" church.

The church was named for the apostle who, along with his brother John, were nicknamed by none other than Jesus the "Sons of Thunder" for their bombastic enthusiasm. That's a good fit for a church serving a neighborhood like Dogtown, with its bigger-than-life Irish character. The parish was founded in 1860 to serve workers in the nearby quarries and brick factories. For years the archdiocese brought priests from Ireland to serve as its pastors. Today, ever in tune with Irish tradition, Mass is celebrated prior to the annual St. Patrick's Day parade before it winds its way through the neighborhood and into some of the city's finest pubs.

By the 1920s, the neighborhood needed a bigger church. The present St. James is a dramatic piece of architecture, designed in the style of 11th-century English Gothic and built of smooth and finely cut ashlar stone. Behind the main altar is an elaborate triptych of woven tapestry, depicting Christ the King surrounded by saints. And, of course, a statue of St. Patrick himself stands off to the side, reminding us of this grand church's link to the Old Sod.

St. John Nepomuk Catholic Church

St. Louis City—Soulard

1625 S 11th St. St. Louis 63104	314.231.0141 Saintjohnnepomuk.org	**MAP LOCATION #19**

A distinct feature of St. Louis is the variety of steeples that define its neighborhoods' skylines. As the 19th-century city absorbed wave after wave of immigrants, each ethnic and national group laid claim to a particular neighborhood and built its own church. It's not unusual for two or more Catholic churches to be located within a few blocks of each other. The spiritual home for St. Louisans of Czech descent is St. John Nepomuk on the city's Near South Side.

Before there was a Czech Republic, there was Bohemia, a small region tucked into the Austro-Hungarian Empire. St. Louis became a refuge for many of its political refugees. In 1854, they established a church in the neighborhood that became known as Bohemian Hill. Named for a 14th-century Bohemian martyr, St. John Nepomuk Church became the center of the neighborhood's social and religious life.

The current structure, built in 1897, is rich with references to its Eastern European heritage in statues, paintings, and stained glass. Inscriptions over doorways and in the Stations of the Cross are written in Czech. The Infant of Prague, a symbol of Bohemian Catholicism and Czech nationalism, occupies a place of honor in the center of the altar.

The neighborhood managed to survive the Civil War, two world wars, the Great Depression, and the Great St. Louis Tornado of 1896, but it was no match for urban renewal and the construction of two interstate highways. Bohemian Hill became largely forgotten as its residents moved, the neighborhood lost its Eastern European flavor, and is today considered a part of the historic Soulard neighborhood.

St. John Nepomuk closed as a parish in 2005 but remains open as a chapel, offering visitors a chance to experience a unique piece of the city's ethnic history and its Catholic faith.

St. John Nepomuk, a remnant of St. Louis's Bohemian neighborhood.

Divine Infant Jesus, I know you love me
and would never leave me.
I thank you for your close presence in my life.

Miraculous Infant, I believe in your promise of
peace, blessings, and freedom from want.
I place every need and care in your hands.

*From Prayer of Thanksgiving
to the Infant of Prague*

Behind the altar of St. John the Apostle and Evangelist is a copy of Raphael's *The Transfiguration*. The original from 1520 is in the Vatican Museum.

St. John the Apostle and Evangelist Catholic Church

St. Louis City—Downtown

15 Plaza Sq.
St. Louis 63103

314.421.3467
Stjohnapostleandevangelist.org

MAP LOCATION #20

St. John's history has been a colorful one since its dedication in 1860. In the early days its location on the edge of the city's sprawling Kerry Patch lent it a distinctly Irish flavor. Its second priest, Father John Bannon of County Roscommon, shocked the archdiocese by leaving his post to serve as a pastor for the Confederate Army. When the riverfront neighborhoods around the Old Cathedral grew jammed with factories and warehouses in the late 1800s, Archbishop Peter Kenrick designated it as the Cathedral Church of the Archdiocese and took up residence next door. His *cathedra*, or bishop's chair, occupies a permanent place in the sanctuary. When nearby Union Station opened

in 1894 as the world's largest train station, the church became a popular place for travelers and downtown workers to worship.

Lovingly restored and in continuous use since the day it opened, St. John's remains a sturdy, brick reminder of St. Louis's past.

A large Celtic cross before its door attests to the church's ethnic heritage.

Infant of Prague

Until you know the story behind it, the small statue of a child dressed like a king might seem strange. The little fellow is called the Infant of Prague, and he looks like a doll. So, why would he occupy a place of honor in a church? His story starts in 16th-century Spain and takes us to Bohemia, through tales of war, the lives of saints, miraculous happenings, and a special way of seeing God.

Long ago in Spain a monk, inspired by a vision, is said to have carved a wooden statue of the Infant Jesus. It eventually turned up in Prague, where a princess donated it to the monastery of Discalced Carmelites. Another version of the story claims that it belonged to the Spanish mystic and Carmelite reformer St. Teresa of Avila. In either case, the wandering statue came to be associated with both the Carmelites and Eastern European Catholicism.

During the Thirty Years' War, invading Swedes drove the Carmelites from the city. When they returned in 1635, a monk found the statue among a pile of rubbish. As he returned it to the monastery's oratory, it spoke to him, saying, "Have mercy on me, and I will have mercy on you. Give me hands, and I will give you peace. The more you honor me, the more I will bless you." Noticing that its hands were broken off, he replaced them, and over the following 300 years, a steady stream of those who pray to the Infant have reported cures and other good fortunes. St. Thérèse de Lisieux, the "Little Flower," was particularly attracted to the Infant's smallness.

Today the elaborately dressed wooden baby, covered with a coat of painted wax, continues to reside in its shrine in the Church of Our Lady of Victory in Prague. Replicas are seen in every part of the world, especially within the Carmelite community and in Czech and Eastern European churches. The Infant's garments are regularly changed, as those of a priest, to correspond to the seasons of the Church Year.

Christianity has a way of turning things on their heads to show us fresh ways to see. The Infant of Prague shows us God not as the bearded elder, but as a vulnerable child, nevertheless capable of bestowing blessings upon us while holding the whole power of the universe in his tiny hands.

Infant of Prague from
Our Lady of Good Counsel in Kansas City.

St. Mary of Victories is home to works
of Catholic art from the past two centuries.

A great sign appeared in the sky,
a woman clothed with the sun,
with the moon under her feet, and on her head
a crown of twelve stars.

Revelation 12:1

St. Mary of Victories Catholic Church

St. Louis City—Chouteau's Landing

744 S 3rd St.　　　　　314.231.8101　　　　　**MAP LOCATION #21**
St. Louis 63102

Tucked among the highway ramps and elevated train tracks that cut through what's left of the riverfront's old factory district is a historical and architectural treasure. The neighborhood has gone through multiple transformations, but St. Mary of Victories remains surprisingly unchanged since 1844, the year it opened as St. Louis's second-oldest Catholic church.

Prior to the Civil War, large numbers of Germans moved into the area called Chouteau's Landing, just south of downtown. The Old Cathedral was the city's sole Catholic church, and German-speaking Catholics wanted their own place to worship. Over the next century it played a major role in the social and religious life of the city's German population. In the 1870s, a small group of nuns arrived from Germany and built a convent adjoining the church. They came to be known as the Sisters of St. Mary, founders of what has become the SSM Health System.

Families of the original immigrants moved to the suburbs after World War II, and, following the 1956 Hungarian uprising against the Soviet Union, the church became the spiritual center for Hungarian refugees. Statues and paintings of St. Stephen, patron saint of Hungary, adorn the church, and parts of the Mass are still conducted in Hungarian.

German craftsmanship of the era is evident in the altars, baptismal font, and Stations of the Cross. The high altar contains one of the region's largest collections of relics.

St. Mary of Victories' roots extend back to the earliest days of the city's Catholic faith. Its quiet space, filled with remnants from the past, remind us of those things that remain unchanged through time.

St. Vincent de Paul

Some of our favorite saints are the ones who are less than perfect. They're easy to like, and they boost our faith that there's hope for the rest of us. Vincent de Paul was grouchy. He admitted it. He was exceptionally bright, but he joined the priesthood because he thought it would be an easy life. The turning point in his spiritual journey came when he heard the confession of a dying peasant. Whatever occurred at that moment sent him on a lifelong mission to serve the poor.

Seventeenth-century France offered little relief for its least fortunate. De Paul worked as a chaplain for galley slaves in Paris. Eventually he assumed leadership of a group of missionaries committed to helping the rural poor. He organized wealthy women in Paris to raise money for missionary projects, hospitals, aid for victims of war, and ransoms for slaves. At a time when the Church was reeling from the Protestant Reformation, de Paul worked to reform the clergy and establish seminaries throughout France.

He was canonized in 1737, and today he is celebrated as the patron saint of charitable works. For Missourians he has particular importance. The missionaries he led in France became known as the Vincentians and brought Catholicism to the region south of St. Louis in the 1820s. From there they spread throughout the state. The Society of Saint Vincent de Paul, established in 1833, was introduced to the United States in 1845 at St. Louis's Old Cathedral. Today it conducts its work in 140 countries.

So, it seems Vincent de Paul was wrong about the priesthood being a cushy job. For that we are grateful. And according to reports from those who knew him, he eventually shed his irascible temperament and grew into a most compassionate and pleasant person. A happy ending.

A blissful St. Vincent in his chapel at St. Louis's Rigali Center.

St. Vincent de Paul Catholic Church

St. Louis City—LaSalle Park

1408 S 10th St. St. Louis 63104	314.231.9328 Stvstl.org	**MAP LOCATION #22**

By the 1840s, Frenchtown, on the city's South Side, was becoming less French and more German. Most of the city's Catholics were worshipping in the Old Cathedral, and it was getting crowded on Sunday mornings. When St. Vincent de Paul was dedicated in 1845, Germans living in Frenchtown finally had a place of their own. Over time, immigrants from Eastern Europe joined them, and what became known as the Soulard neighborhood grew into a bustling, diverse part of the city.

As its name suggests, St. Vincent de Paul was built and run by the Vincentians, the order that spread Catholicism throughout the territory south of St. Louis. The church was designed by architect George Barnett, who also created St. Louis's Old Courthouse, the Grand Avenue Water Tower, Henry Shaw's home in Tower Grove Park, and the Missouri Governor's Mansion.

Today an interstate highway passes within yards of its old façade. The surrounding blocks are a mix of industry and historical architecture in various stages of renovation. The church's interior retains its 19th-century charm. Stained glass transforms daylight into colored shadows. Saints and angels watch from their posts in the sanctuary. Christ hangs upon his cross. Time passes gently here.

A painting of the Holy Trinity fills the apse.

An Angel weeps at the main altar of St. Vincent de Paul.

Dear God, You filled Vincent de Paul
with the strength of the apostles
to work for the salvation of the poor.

May we who follow the example of his life
be driven by unceasing charity to continue
the mission of Your Son in the world.

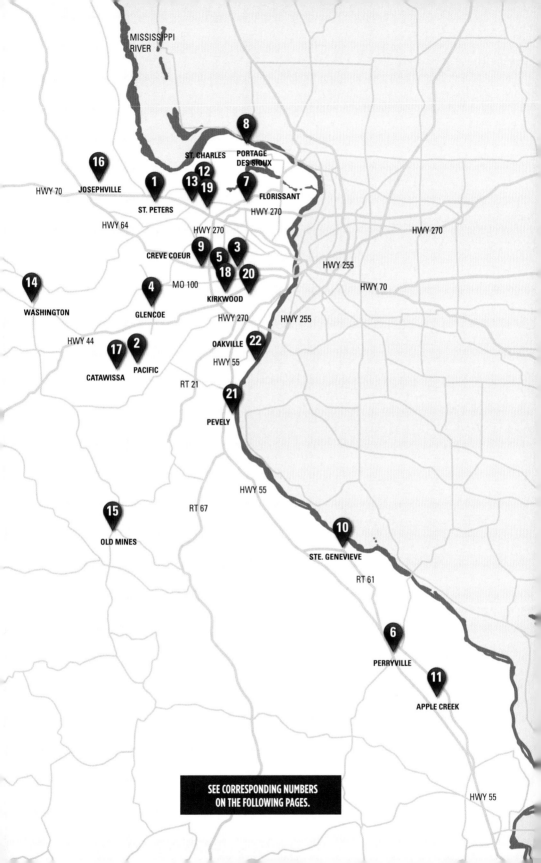

MISSISSIPPI RIVER

16 JOSEPHVILLE

HWY 70

1 ST. PETERS

13 **12** **19**

ST. CHARLES

8

PORTAGE DES SIOUX

7 FLORISSANT

HWY 270

HWY 64

HWY 270

HWY 270

CREVE COEUR

9

5 **3**

18 **20**

KIRKWOOD

HWY 255

HWY 70

14 WASHINGTON

4 GLENCOE

MO 100

HWY 270

HWY 255

HWY 44

17 **2**

CATAWISSA PACIFIC

OAKVILLE **22**

HWY 55

RT 21

21 PEVELY

HWY 55

RT 67

15 OLD MINES

10 STE. GENEVIEVE

RT 61

6 PERRYVILLE

11 APPLE CREEK

SEE CORRESPONDING NUMBERS
ON THE FOLLOWING PAGES.

HWY 55

Archdiocese
of St. Louis
BEYOND THE CITY

St. Anne and her daughter Mary stand beside the altar of All Saints Church.

St. Anne
with child Mary

All Saints Catholic Church

St. Peters

7 McMenamy Rd.　　　636.397.1440　　　MAP LOCATION #1
St. Peters 63376　　　Allsaints-stpeters.org

It wasn't so long ago that you knew you were passing the sleepy little town of St. Peters off Interstate 70 when the silhouette of All Saints Church revealed itself from a distant hill. That was before St. Peters ballooned into a city of 57,000 people. Today the church is a remnant of quieter days, holding the strip malls at bay.

In 1823, a small group of French Canadians began celebrating Mass in the area. They called their church St. Peters and named the village Dardenne, after the local creek. By 1856, the region was mostly German, the town was called St. Peters, and the church was renamed All Saints. The current church was completed in 1882, built in the Gothic style so beloved by Missouri's Germans.

The graveyard and a grotto of Our Lady of Lourdes are just a short walk from the front steps of the church. The busy streets of modern St. Peters are just a few blocks away, and the highway hums in the background, but this historic place on the top of the hill has managed to hold onto the peaceful atmosphere of an earlier time.

A spiritual home for generations.

Black Madonna Shrine and Grottos

Pacific

100 St. Joseph Hill Rd.   636.938.5361   MAP LOCATION #2
Pacific 63069

The collection of weather-worn grottos on the grounds of the Black Madonna Shrine evokes a sense of a distant past. It's a scene where thousands of stones are arranged for a holy purpose in a forest clearing, and their story is a testament to love and sacrifice.

In 1927, a group of Franciscan monks emigrated from Poland to an area outside Pacific to build an infirmary. After several years, one of the brothers, Bronislaus Luszcz, was inspired to clear a space in the nearby woods and build a chapel. Above the altar he hung a portrait of the Black Madonna of Częstochowa and dedicated it to the Queen of Peace and Mercy. The Black Madonna is an ancient and revered image, particularly in Eastern Europe, with a history richly decorated with legend.

Beginning in 1937, Brother Bronislaus began what would become his lifelong task of single-handedly building a collection of grottos to house statues of the Virgin Mary, Jesus and the disciples, the Nativity, the Crucifixion, St. Francis, St. Joseph, and other holy images. Among the stones he embedded colored jars, seashells, costume jewelry, ceramic figurines, and gifts left by pilgrims.

He labored on his act of love for 23 years, until he died of heat exhaustion while working on a grotto for Our Lady of Fatima. A seashell marks the place of his death. The demonstration of his faith, in each rock placed upon another, offers us inspiration for our own prayers.

The shrine's chapel offers visitors a place to pray before the beloved icon.

A foggy morning on the grounds of the Black Madonna Shrine and Grottos.

Holy Mother of Częstochowa,
Thou art full of grace, goodness, and mercy.

I consecrate to Thee all my thoughts, words,
and actions, my soul and body.

I beseech Thy blessings and
especially prayers for my salvation.

Prayer to the Black Madonna

The Black Madonna
of Częstochowa

It's no surprise that Brother Bronislaus would devote his life to building a shrine for the Black Madonna. There is no icon more revered in Eastern Europe or blessed with a richer history of mystery and legend. The painting of a dark-complected Holy Mother and Infant Jesus has inspired a genre of similar images that occupy shrines and churches around the world.

The Black Madonna found its current home in the monastery of Jasna Gora in the Polish city of Częstochowa over 600 years ago. Legend credits St. Luke as the original artist, who painted it on wood from a table built by Jesus. It's said that in the fourth century, St. Helena found it in Jerusalem while searching for the True Cross and gave it to her son, Constantine the Great. Modern art historians have constructed a considerably less romantic provenance, attributing its origin to sometime between the sixth and ninth centuries.

The Madonna bears two scars on her right cheek, which have their own place in legend. In 1430, a Protestant army stormed the monastery and tossed the artwork into a wagon with their other plunder. When their horses refused to move, an angry soldier threw the painting to the ground and slashed it twice with his sword before being struck dead. It's said that ever since, restorers have repeatedly failed to remove the blemishes.

In the 17th century, the image was credited with saving the monastery from a Swedish siege, in which 180 Poles and 7 monks held off an army of 40,000.

But why a Black Madonna? Particularly in a predominantly white Europe where the image of a fair-skinned Mary has long been the popular favorite? Theories abound. Some church authorities have offered the explanation that her darkness is unintentional, the result of centuries of candle smoke and deteriorating paint. But if that were the case, wouldn't we see a lot more Black saints? More credible is the explanation that an artist living in Eastern Europe over a thousand years ago was able to imagine Mary as who she was, a woman from the Middle East.

There are other theories inspired by Christianity's history of adapting pagan influences to its own traditions. The ancient world is full of Black, religious deities, their darkness often associated with the earth and fertility. The Black Madonna might be an echo of earlier beliefs.

Perhaps forensic science and art history are simply not up to the task of explaining why the Black Madonna is Black, or why she is so adored and imitated. But there is power in mystery, and maybe this mother and son are not intended to be so easily understood.

An icon with a mysterious and miraculous past.

The Chapel of the Precious Blood is
open to visitors from morning to evening.

Chapel of the Precious Blood, Carmel of St. Joseph

Ladue

9150 Clayton Rd. Ladue 63124	314.993.6899 Stlouiscarmel.com	**MAP LOCATION #3**

The Discalced Carmelite nuns, while devoted to a life of prayer and solitude, make their chapel available to everyone. Discalced means "shoeless," and it refers to their tradition of wearing open sandals as an expression of humility. Though cloistered, they regard their convent as a garden of faith, connecting Heaven and earth.

Their tradition began in the 12th century with a group of hermits who settled on Mount Carmel in the Holy Land to live a simple life of prayer and dedication to the Holy Mother. When the order spread, each of their monasteries was considered its own Carmel. The following centuries brought turmoil throughout Europe and within the Church, and in the 16th century St. Teresa founded an even more disciplined branch of the Carmelite family in Avila, Spain. She called her convent the St. Joseph Carmel.

In 1863, five Discalced sisters arrived in St. Louis to pray for the priests of the archdiocese. By 1878, they had their own brick convent in a building that still stands perched above the depressed lanes of Interstate 55. In 1928, they built their current home on a piece of land on Clayton Road in what's today the St. Louis suburb of Ladue.

A small community of cloistered sisters shares its days together, centered on prayer, Eucharistic Adoration, work, and devotion to Mary. Except for designated times when conversation is permitted, they are bound to silence. In stillness they find fullness, like Elijah, who on Mount Horeb experienced God not in a storm, an earthquake, or flashes of fire, but in a gentle whisper.

Let nothing disturb you,
let nothing frighten you,
all things will pass away.

God never changes;
patience obtains all things,
whoever has God lacks nothing.
God alone suffices.

Prayer of St. Teresa of Avila

By living holy lives, dedicated to God's love, the Carmelite nuns aim to do no less than transform the world. The door to their chapel is open, an invitation for the world to share that mission.

The Sacred Heart Grotto is one of many quiet spaces located on the grounds of the La Salle Retreat Center.

La Salle Retreat Center

Glencoe

2101 Rue de La Salle Dr.   636.938.5374   **MAP LOCATION #4**
Glencoe 63038   Lasalleretreat.org

It's surprising that a place so close to metropolitan St. Louis could feel so peacefully isolated from the city's noise and confusion. The collection of old buildings perched on a hilltop overlooking the highway is clearly from a time long passed. In the 1870s, the site was an orphanage and an industrial school for boys. In 1886, the Christian Brothers repurposed it into a center for young men studying to join the order.

Over the years it grew into a self-sufficient community, spread over 800 acres. More than 200 novices and brothers raised farm animals and tended gardens at what soon became recognized as a premier educational institution. Disaster was averted in the 1930s when the state planned to run the highway directly through its grounds. Prayers to St. Joseph and a well-executed lobbying effort produced the miracle they needed.

In 1978, the grounds became a retreat center, welcoming individuals and groups to come and find quiet places to meet with God. Its wooded hills and open, grassy spaces are connected by paths taking visitors past shrines, grottos, and Stations of the Cross. Many retreatants walk its labyrinth, which has no wrong turns for those who wander its bends and curves, reflecting on the greater path God has in mind for them.

Mercy Conference
and Retreat Center

Frontenac

2039 N Geyer Rd.
Frontenac 63131

314.966.4686
Mercycenterstl.org

MAP LOCATION #5

The Sisters of Mercy have devoted themselves to serving the poor since they took their first vows in Dublin in 1831. Upon arriving in St. Louis shortly before the Civil War, they immediately began establishing orphanages, schools, and hospitals for the city's impoverished immigrant communities. The condition of women and children has always been of particular concern to them, and they continue to this day to play an active role in the life of the community.

In that same tradition, the Sisters operate a facility in St. Louis County devoted to the spiritual and mental health of people of all faiths. The spacious grounds are an ideal setting for visitors to relax and seek peace and tranquility. Paths wind through wooded areas. Stations of the Cross, a grotto to Our Lady of Lourdes, and a labyrinth invite visitors to prayer and meditation. Individuals or groups are welcome, and services include spiritual direction, creative spirituality workshops, and healing through massage.

At the heart of the center is a chapel in the round, accented with a sweep of colorful stained glass windows depicting works of mercy. Its clean and simple lines and contemporary liturgical art communicate the simple honesty of modern design, creating its own sense of peace.

The center describes itself as "a place to follow the deep human longing to come away for a while, to find a place apart in which to connect more deeply with God, nature, and community."

The chapel is designed in the style of mid-century modern.

> You, Lord, give perfect peace to those who keep their purpose firm and put their trust in you.
>
> ---
>
> *Isaiah 26:3*

St. Thérèse de Lisieux

(The Little Flower)

Marie Francoise-Thérèse Martin performed no great deeds in her short life. When she died of tuberculosis at the age of 24, it did not occur to her Carmelite sisters that she would be remembered as one of the most venerated saints in the history of the Church.

She knew she would become a nun from the time she was a child growing up in a small French village. She was only 15 years old when she entered the convent, fairly bursting with the intention of demonstrating her love for God in great and dramatic ways. Instead, she grew ever more aware of her smallness. It was a painful realization until she came to understand that her insignificance didn't have to be an obstacle to showing her love for God. On the contrary, it would be her path. She called it "the small way." It was because she was little and in need of help that Jesus would carry her, like a child, to holiness. She considered herself to be like a little flower, and from that point on, it was not necessary to seek signs from God. Her trust would be enough.

In the last days of her life she wrote, "After my death, I will let fall a shower of roses. I will spend my heaven doing good upon earth. I will raise up a mighty host of little saints. My mission is to make God loved." She left behind a spiritual autobiography, *The Story of a Soul*, which popularized her simple approach. Stories spread—and continue to be told today—of how those praying to her would see roses or smell their fragrance.

There are many reasons St. Thérèse de Lisieux appeals so strongly to us today. In the realm of saints, she's relatively close to us in time. Unlike many of her predecessors, we have photographs of her which reveal a genuine sweetness in her face. In our complicated world, we welcome her message of simplicity. We look for signs; she tells us it's not necessary. Trust is enough. We feel small, and she tells us that's the point. Welcome, she says, to her small way.

St. Thérèse de Lisieux scatters roses upon earth from her place in Heaven. Statue in St. Louis's New Cathedral.

The splendor of the rose and the whiteness of the lily
do not rob the little violet of its scent nor the daisy of its simple charm.

If every tiny flower wanted to be a rose,
spring would lose its loveliness.

St. Thérèse de Lisieux

Shrine of the Miraculous Medal
in St. Mary of the Barrens.

O Mary conceived without sin,
pray for us who have
recourse to thee.

—

*Inscription on the medal,
as communicated to
Sister Catherine Laboure*

National Shrine of Our Lady of the Miraculous Medal

Perryville

1805 W St. Joseph St.   800.264.6279   **MAP LOCATION #6**
Perryville 63775   Amm.org

In 1818, a cluster of Catholic families living in southern Missouri offered land to a group of French Vincentian priests to serve their spiritual needs and establish a seminary. In 1827, they laid the cornerstone for St. Mary's of the Barren, which remains today a source of pride for the town of Perryville.

At about the same time, Catherine Laboure, a novice of the Daughters of Charity in Paris, received a series of visits from the Virgin Mary, who presented her with a design for a medal and instructions to have it cast so the entire world could receive it.

The first medal was struck in 1832, and its popularity spread quickly from France to the rest of the world, as cures for both body and soul were attributed to it. In 1929, St. Mary's of the Barren became the site of the National Shrine of Our Lady of the Miraculous Medal.

For all its miraculous attributes, the medal is not a good luck charm. It doesn't have magic powers. It is, as the Church describes it, a prayer in the form of a medal. A visit to the shrine is a chance to reflect on history, appreciate the artistic treasures of the church, enjoy the lush beauty of the grounds, and reflect upon the possibilities of miracles.

Medal of Mary, inspired by a vision.

Old St. Ferdinand Church and Shrine

Florissant

1 Rue St. Francois
Florissant 63031

314.837.2110
Oldstferdinandshrine.com

MAP LOCATION #7

A visit to Old St. Ferdinand in Florissant is a trip through time to the earliest days of Catholic Missouri. The convent was built in 1819. The church has stood beside it since 1821 and is the oldest existing church in what was the Louisiana Territory. They built the rectory in 1840. The 1888 schoolhouse is the relative newcomer to the scene.

When the parish of St. Ferdinand was established in 1789, the area around present-day Florissant was a cluster of French plantations under Spanish rule. The Spanish called it St. Ferdinand; the French, Fleurissant. Long before it became a part of the United States, it was a place where European colonial, indigenous, and American cultures intersected to create a new frontier society.

The site is a time capsule. As you walk through the old buildings and view the many artifacts and relics on display, the past seems very close. Saint Rose Philippine Duchesne made St. Ferdinand her home for years when she wasn't living in St. Charles or among the Potawatomi. Her room in the convent, a small closet beneath the stairway, is still there, and the confessional where she sought absolution for her sins (which couldn't have been many) still stands along the back wall. The great Jesuit missionary Pierre-Jean De Smet was ordained at the church in 1827, and explorers Meriwether Lewis and William Clark attended a wedding there. Encased in glass below the altar is a wax effigy of the third-century Roman Saint Valentine, containing a small collection of his bones.

Mass is still celebrated in the church, and it's open to visitors for prayer, though it hasn't been a parish church since the 1950s. When Saint Rose was canonized in 1988, the archdiocese declared the complex a shrine. Today the historic site is operated by a friends' group that preserves these architectural and historical treasures so that we can walk in the footsteps of a saint and experience the essence of a time long passed.

Beneath the altar of Old Ferdinand is a relic of St. Valentine, a gift from the King of France.

Lord, Jesus, through the intercession
of St. Rose Philippine Duchesne,
to your Sacred Heart confide (this intention).

Only look.
Then do what your Heart inspires.
Let your heart decide.
I count on It. I trust in It.
I throw myself at Its Mercy.

Lord Jesus, You will not fail me!

Novena of Confidence

The Shrine of Our Lady of the Rivers
is visible for miles along the banks of the Mississippi.

Our Lady of the Rivers Shrine

Portage des Sioux

1553 River View Dr.
Portage des Sioux 63373   Ourladyoftheriversshrine.org

MAP LOCATION #8

Portage des Sioux is a tiny village with a long history. Three great rivers—the Mississippi, Missouri, and Illinois—intersect not far to its north. It got its name when French settlers observed native tribes hauling their canoes overland as a shortcut between the Mississippi and the Missouri rivers. For centuries, a variety of cultures have crossed paths there—Sac, Fox, Osage, Sioux, French, Spanish, British, and American—as they competed for control of the rivers.

In 1951, a massive flood threatened to wash the town away. As the waters crept into the streets, the pastor at St. Francis of Assisi asked his parishioners to pray to Mary to intercede. When the waters receded, they built a shrine devoted to Our Lady in gratitude for their answered prayers. A crowd of 10,000 turned out for the dedication in October of 1957.

The 25-foot fiberglass statue of Our Lady of the Rivers has a mid-century, streamlined elegance. Rising from a 20-foot pedestal, it's visible from the Illinois shore for miles. It's so large that the closer you get, the more difficult it becomes to take it all in. Your eyes look past it to the endless flow of this gigantic river and the bluffs it carved along the distant shore. It's as if Our Lady directs you to focus on the power of God's Creation, respect its unpredictability, and experience a touch of humility.

> Remember, O most gracious Virgin Mary, that never was it known that any one who fled to your protection, implored your help, or sought your intercession, was left unaided.
>
> Inspired with this confidence, I fly unto you, O Virgin of virgins, my Mother. To you I come; before you I stand, sinful and sorrowful.
>
> O Mother of the Word Incarnate, despise not my petitions, but in your mercy hear and answer me. Amen.
>
> ---
>
> *Prayer by Saint Bernard of Clairvaux on the pedestal of Our Lady of the Rivers Shrine*

Saint Louis Abbey

Creve Coeur

500 S Mason Rd.   314.434.3690   **MAP LOCATION #9**
Creve Coeur 63141   Stlouisabbey.org

In 1955, a group of St. Louis lay Catholics invited three Benedictine monks from Ampleforth Abbey in Yorkshire to open a boys' school based on the English Benedictine educational tradition. The brothers established a monastery in west St. Louis County and founded Saint Louis Priory School.

In 1962, the monks opened the Abbey Church, St. Anselm. Even by the standards of modern church architecture, it was something special. It was designed by Gyo Obata, whose architectural creations would earn him international fame. The exterior of the church consists of three stacked tiers of thin concrete parabolic arches, the top one serving as a bell tower. The arches create an illusion of lightness, as if they might catch the wind and sail like a kite.

From the outside the windows appear to be black. From inside they are translucent, like alabaster, revealing the world beyond its walls as a place of shadows. The mood is one of calmness, its white walls, ceramic floor, and oak pews coexisting in a harmony of color and texture. At certain times of the day the granite altar glows softly under light filtering in through the bell tower. The acoustics lend the space a unique brand of silence.

Beyond the serenity of the chapel, the monastery grounds are a busy place. The brothers live according to the Benedictine discipline of prayer and work but are never too busy to welcome strangers.

The circular space brings a sense of community and intimacy to the Mass.

A 14th-century French statue of the Madonna and Child is quite at home in the Abbey's 20th-century church.

Gracious and Holy Father,
give us the wisdom to discover You,
the intelligence to understand You,
the diligence to seek after You,
the patience to wait for You,
eyes to behold You,
a heart to meditate upon You,
and a life to proclaim You,
through the power of the Spirit of Jesus, our Lord.

St. Benedict

The main altar of Ste. Genevieve, where church and town share two centuries of history.

Sainte Genevieve, you who cured the sick and fed the hungry,
obtain the light of God and make us stronger to reject temptation.

You who had the concern of the poor,
protect the sick, abandoned, and the unemployed.

Give us the direction for truth and justice.
Help us to keep the teachings of our Lord Jesus Christ.

May your example be for us an encouragement
to always seek God and serve Him through our brothers and sisters.

Sainte Genevieve Catholic Church

Ste. Genevieve

49 Dubourg Pl.
Ste. Genevieve 63670

573.883.2731
Stegenevieveparish.com

MAP LOCATION #10

Missouri towns simply don't get more French than Ste. Genevieve. Bearing the name of the fifth-century mystic and patron saint of Paris, it has lovingly preserved its past for more than two centuries. Many of the original 18th-century houses still stand along its narrow streets, reminding visitors of its heritage.

A Catholic church has occupied the same plot in the heart of town since a simple log church was built there in the 1790s. It was replaced by a stone structure in the 1830s, which was dismantled after the current church was built around it in the late 1870s. Pieces of the foundations from the first two churches are still visible in the basement.

This church and this town have shared a long and unbroken history. The steeple and bell tower are visible from every corner of the town. The oldest of its four bells was cast in 1847 and named after St. Joseph, patron of the happy death. It is a local tradition to ring it when a parishioner dies so that the entire town can take a moment for a memory or a prayer. The baptistry in the chapel contains a stone bowl, claimed to be from the first log church. Several of the town's earliest citizens are buried beneath the altar, and the church is the steward of many relics, including one from Ste. Genevieve herself.

God has been listening to prayers for a very long time from this small place with the big history. There's good reason to believe that yours will be heard as well.

The Annunciation in stained glass.

Divine Mercy

As you visit various holy sites throughout Missouri, you'll often see copies of a particular painting of Jesus. It depicts him taking a step toward the viewer as he raises his right hand. Rays of red and white light stream forth from his heart. It's known as the Divine Mercy, and its story has inspired worldwide devotion.

The story begins with Sister Faustina Kowalska, a Polish nun and mystic. Throughout her life she experienced visions of Jesus, and in December of 1931, He appeared to her wearing a white robe with red and clear rays (signifying blood and water) emanating from his heart. He asked that a painting be made of him in the way he appeared to her, signed with the words, "Jesus, I trust in You," promising that "the soul that will venerate this image will not perish."

There were obstacles. The priest assigned as her confessor was not convinced and had her undergo an extensive psychiatric examination, which she handily passed. Also, Sr. Faustina was not a painter. In time her confessor came to believe her and arranged for her to work with a local artist, Eugene Kazimierowski, to translate her vision to canvas. When she saw the completed work in 1934, she wept because, she said, it didn't capture the beauty of her experience.

Sr. Faustina continued to have conversations with Jesus. He asked her to "proclaim that mercy is the greatest attribute of God" and to create a chaplet that could be said on Rosary beads. The prayer would ask for God's mercy, trust in Christ's endless goodness, and dedication to serving as conduits for God's love by showing mercy to others.

Before her death in 1938 at the age of 33, she predicted "a terrible, terrible war," and in the following years devotion to Divine Mercy spread throughout war-ravaged Poland. After the war, Polish artist Adolf Hyla, in gratitude for his survival, painted a new version of the Divine Mercy image, which has grown even more popular than the original. Today artists continue to create new versions, inspired by Sr. Faustina's visions.

As a Polish native, St. John Paul II had great affection for the devotion and arranged for the Feast of the Divine Mercy to be celebrated on the first Sunday after Easter. He expressed his feelings simply and elegantly: "Apart from the mercy of God, there is no other source of hope for mankind."

Image of Divine Mercy beside
a road near New Haven.

Eternal God, in whom mercy is endless
and the treasury of compassion inexhaustible,
look kindly upon us and increase Your mercy in us,
that in difficult moments we might not despair nor become despondent,
but with great confidence submit ourselves to Your holy will,
which is Love and Mercy itself.

Closing prayer, Chaplet of Divine Mercy

Shrine of Our Lady of Grace

Apple Creek

138 St. Joseph Ln.   573.788.2330   **MAP LOCATION #11**
Apple Creek 63775

While you're visiting Our Lady of the Miraculous Medal in Perryville, you might drive about 10 miles down Highway 61 and visit Apple Creek, home to a remarkable shrine created around a rare and beautiful natural formation.

Apple Creek's first settlers were German Catholics who arrived in southern Missouri in the 1820s via New Orleans. In the early years, priests from Perryville celebrated Mass in a log church named for St. Joseph. The present church was dedicated in 1884, and in its graveyard rest the remains of generations of parishioners. A path leads from the church down a hill to a spring, which has provided the town with fresh water for the past two centuries.

The spring is part of an unusual geological phenomenon. It flows through an underground cave but is visible where a portion of its roof collapsed long ago. The formation of rock and stone seemed the perfect place for a shrine. In the 1950s, parishioners constructed an elaborate grotto of stones taken from the foundations of abandoned farmhouses and barns. Today a waterfall pours from the cave into a pool, past an altar, beneath a small bridge, and back into the cave. Atop a wooded hill is a statue to Our Lady of Grace.

It's a wonder of nature and of human labor, inspired by faith, and enhanced by the songs of birds and the rush of water.

Shrine of Saint Rose Philippine Duchesne

St. Charles

619 N 2nd St.   314.750.8429   **MAP LOCATION #12**
St. Charles 63301   Rsj.org

It was the lure of missionary work in the New World that prompted Sr. Rose Philippine Duchesne to make the difficult journey from her home in France to the Missouri Territory. In 1818, she founded a Sacred Heart convent and school in St. Charles, and for the next 35 years she opened schools across the American frontier. Her many years of serving native tribes earned her the Potawatomi title of *Quahkahkanumad*, "The Woman Who Prays Always." Finally exhausted by the hardships of frontier life, she returned to St. Charles and moved into a tiny room at the convent until her death in 1852.

Her shrine is located on the site of the original convent, two blocks from the river on the edge of the city's historic district. Built and rebuilt throughout the 1950s and '60s, it's surrounded by many of the original brick structures as well as a modern elementary school. The interior of the shrine is open and spacious, incorporating a blend of modernist and traditional Catholic design. During the day, colored light from stained glass windows plays on the floors and walls. A marble sarcophagus containing the saint's remains rests beneath a wooden crucifix from the school where, as a young girl, she first received her religious calling.

Past and present exist comfortably together at the Shrine of Saint Rose Philippine Duchesne, a tribute to a remarkable woman whose presence is still felt in this place where she first set foot over 200 years ago.

Shrine of Saint Rose Philippine Duchesne in downtown St. Charles.

St. Charles Borromeo Catholic Church

St. Charles

601 N 4th St.　　　　　636.946.1893　　　　　**MAP LOCATION #13**
St. Charles 63301　　　Borromeoparish.com

It's a short walk from the Shrine of Saint Rose Philippine Duchesne
to St. Charles Borromeo Church, a solid stone structure bearing some
similarity to a medieval fortress. The histories of the church and the
town are closely entwined. Originally called Les Petites Cotes (the little
hills), the town took the name of St. Charles after the first log church
was established in 1791 and dedicated to the Italian saint Charles
Borromeo. The town's other saint, Sister Rose, was a latecomer; she
didn't arrive until 1818.

The current church, the parish's fourth, was dedicated in 1917,
but despite its relative newness looks as if it's been standing there forever.
Its interior is spacious and softly lit from stained glass windows set high
in the walls. The colors of the pillars and arched walls are warm and
subdued, creating a quiet, peaceful mood. Items from previous churches
adorn the space, and a statue of St. Rose tucked into a corner reminds
us of her role in the stories of town and church.

St. Charles places high value on its past. A reconstruction of
the first log church stands on its original site on Main Street.
Memorials of all kinds refer to its history as a launching site for

European settlement
of the continent and its
origins as a Catholic
city on the banks of the
Missouri. St. Charles
Borromeo captures the
spirit of that tradition.

A majestic beauty.

St. Rose Philippine Duchesne occupies a quiet corner of St. Charles Borromeo.

SIMON CARRIE

God the Father, angels, and the Holy Spirit look down from the altar of St. Francis Borgia.

St. Francis Borgia Catholic Church

Washington

115 Cedar St.   636.239.6701   MAP LOCATION #14
Washington 63090   Sfbparish.org

Rising from a steep slope just a block from the Missouri River, St. Francis Borgia is visible from most of historic downtown Washington. Steps descend from its front door to the town below, like a church in an old European city.

The stories of Washington and its Catholic church have been closely entwined for almost 200 years. The town was little more than a scattering of log cabins in 1833 when a dozen German families settled there. The main attraction was the surrounding countryside's similarity to their homeland, and within a few years an influx of immigrants gave the town a distinctly German flavor. For those wondering why a German church is named after a Spanish saint, the answer lies in the Spanish roots of its Jesuit founders.

The little river town expanded quickly as America pushed West. The parish outgrew two churches before the current one opened in 1866. Its interior has undergone several renovations since the turn of the 20th century, but it retains a certain Old World feel. Above the altar, angels surround an image of God Himself reaching with big, outstretched hands to the congregation. Paintings of 11 apostles look down from the arched ceiling. Stained glass windows portray scenes from the Gospels. A large rose window above the choir loft depicts St. Cecilia, patron saint of musicians.

Time has been kind to Washington, Missouri. Its past is well-preserved in the blocks of red brick shops and houses along the river. It's easy to see how this town and its Catholic church on the hill have grown together through so much history over so many years.

> They are like trees that grow beside a stream,
> that bear fruit at the right time, and whose leaves do not dry up.
> They succeed in everything they do.
>
> *Psalm 3:1*

St. Joachim Catholic Church

Old Mines

10120 Crest Rd.	573.438.6181	MAP LOCATION #15
Old Mines 63630	Stjoachim.org	

The names on the headstones in the old St. Joachim Cemetery are mostly French with a healthy sprinkling of Irish. Almost 300 years ago, French settlers arrived here. The Irish showed up later to work in the lead mines that gave the town its economic life and its name. Paved roads didn't come to this part of the state until the 1920s. Log cabins can still be found in the woods outside of town. This is a part of Missouri isolated for so long that well into the 20th century many residents of Old Mines still spoke an antiquated French dialect.

Predominantly Catholic, the early settlers built a log church in Old Mines in 1820. They named it after St. Joachim, the husband of St. Anne and father of Mary. The current church today was constructed in 1831. That makes it three years older than St. Louis's Old Cathedral.

Parishioners expanded it in the 1850s, but since then it hasn't changed much. It's simply and neatly adorned, a dignified country

church, rich in traditions remembered and passed on by its close-knit congregation. It remains today a vital center of community life and culture.

Spiritual center of Old Mines since 1831.

St. Joachim Cemetery.

Relics

Even among the best of Catholics, the veneration of relics is sometimes problematic. For some Protestants, it's just more evidence that Catholics are out of their minds. It's understandable that to some people it might seem ghoulish to take a piece of someone's dead body and put it on display. To make it seem even stranger, the Church has three categories of relics—parts of saints' bodies, items worn or touched by a saint, and items that have physically touched relics from the first two categories. So, how are we supposed to think about this?

Like so many practices of the Church, the meaning is woven into a colorful fabric of history and tradition. References to mystical healing powers appear in the Book of Kings, where a dead man is brought back to life upon touching the bones of the prophet Elisha. The charred bones of the martyred St. Polycarp were preserved and venerated after his execution in the year 156. In the Gospel of Mark, a hemorrhaging woman is healed when she touches Jesus's garment.

The practice gained steam over the centuries. Constantine built basilicas over the remains of Saints Peter and Paul. By the 12th century the trading of relics had grown into an international industry. Imbued with the power to cure the sick, win wars, and prevent plague, famine, and drought, the property and bodies of the blessed were in high demand.

Relic fever has cooled, but it's not unusual today for a church or shrine to display a relic. Every Catholic church has one imbedded in its altar, kissed by the priest before the celebration of the Eucharist. The Shroud of Turin holds the interest of believers and the scientific community. But most 21st-century Catholics don't share their ancestors' view of relics as talismans generating their own supernatural powers. Relics don't perform miracles; God does.

That is not to say relics don't have power, value, or meaning in our modern world. They help get us past the abstract notion of saints as little gods and remind us of their humanity. They connect the physical and the spiritual, the past and the present. It's not so different from the way we feel about the clothing or personal items belonging to someone we have loved and lost, items left behind to help us remember them. And on our way to finding God, don't we really need all the help we can get?

A relic is embedded in the primary altar of every Catholic Church. Altar of St. John the Baptist-Gildehaus in Villa Ridge.

St. Joseph Church, where the craftsmanship of its original German parishioners is still evident.

Hail, Guardian of the Redeemer,
Spouse of the Blessed Virgin Mary.
To you God entrusted His only Son;
In you Mary placed her trust;
with you Christ became man.

Blessed Joseph, to us too,
show yourself a father
and guide us in the path of life.
Obtain for us grace, mercy, and courage,
and defend us from every evil.

St. Joseph Catholic Church

Josephville

1390 Josephville Rd.   636.332.6676   **MAP LOCATION #16**
Josephville 63385   Stjojo.net

Parishioners refer to St. Joseph as "the oldest homemade church in the area." For good reason. When the mostly German congregation outgrew its old log church, parishioners cut lumber from local farms, dug clay, and baked it into bricks for a new church. Its dedication in 1872 was evidence that God smiled upon Josephville and its citizens, many of whom lie today in the carefully tended graveyard just a short walk from the rectory.

There is an air of mystery to a mural above the altar. According to local legend, an artist unexpectedly showed up at the door and offered to create a painting above the altar depicting the death of St. Joseph. After finishing it, he disappeared without asking for a fee

or signing his work. It was restored in the 1990s and to this day teases the question of whether St. Joseph Church might once have been specially touched by the Divine.

Painting above the altar
depicts the death of St. Joseph.

St. Patrick of Armagh Catholic Church

Catawissa

150 Rock Church Rd.
Catawissa 63015   Stpatricksorc.org

MAP LOCATION #17

This tiny limestone church is steeped in Missouri history, and even though it's only open for special events, the "Rock Church," as it's commonly called, is worth a visit. Irish railroad workers named it after their patron saint and the city of his first church. The town got its name from the original home of the Pennsylvania stone workers who built the church.

History is built into the walls themselves. The first few feet of stone, quarried near the site and set in place in 1861, were so finely cut that they fit together without need of mortar. The Civil War halted construction, but when it resumed, the stones were still artfully but more quickly cut and set with mortar. The walls withstood a fire in 1885, after which workmen rebuilt the roof and interior.

Constructed by people facing the daily challenge of surviving in a remote part of postwar Missouri, the church is rich with architectural details that testify to the importance they placed in it. The roof is an engineering marvel, incorporating a system of interlocked beams and planks fitted tightly together without need of nails. A recurring theme of Gothic arches in the windows, communion rails, and paneling brings a sense of lightness to the interior and a nod to history.

From its earliest days St. Patrick, because of its isolation and a local spirit of tolerance, was a gathering place for both Catholics and Protestants. That tradition continues today with its annual summer picnic, bringing together visitors from the entire region to support this simple but exquisite remnant of rural Catholicism.

Masters of Glass

Emil Frei and Associates

Stained glass designs have occupied the windows of Catholic churches since the seventh century. In the days before most of our ancestors could read, images in glass helped them imagine events and personalities described in the Scriptures. They transform daylight into colors as we rarely see them, separating us from our ordinary world and creating moods that play to our imaginations. For over a century, some of the world's most beautifully crafted stained glass has been created by a St. Louis company named for its founder, Emil Frei. As you visit churches throughout Missouri, you'll certainly see examples of its work.

Emil Frei Sr. emigrated from Bavaria and set up a studio in St. Louis around 1900. He introduced the highly detailed, pictorial style of Munich glass to the city at a time when many grand churches were being constructed to accommodate the influx of Catholic, European immigrants.

Among the company's early works are windows for Saint Louis University's College Church, St. Francis de Sales, and mosaics for the New Cathedral. His son, Emil Frei Jr., pioneered modern, liturgical art and attracted a collection of artists who broadened the company's creative scope and introduced styles and lines to fit the tastes of the postwar years. The windows of many suburban, mid-century churches across the country, and particularly in St. Louis, feature Frei glass.

The studio continues to expand the boundaries of liturgical art. Their designs are appreciated for their sophisticated understanding of theology and their grasp of the creative possibilities of glass as a design material. Today, the fifth generation of Frei family glass artists create works for churches, hospitals, seminaries, and religious centers of various faiths around the world. Sometimes they're called upon to restore a piece created by their great-great-grandfather. Their talent for adapting the inspirational powers of an ancient genre to the sensibilities of a modern world is a God-given gift, passed through their family to an appreciative world.

Window for the Shrine of
Our Lady of Sorrows in Starkenburg.
Photo, Emil Frei and Associates.

IN PIAM MEM. REV. DOM NI FRANCISCI BOEHM.

St. Peter Catholic Church

Kirkwood

243 W Argonne Dr.   314.966.8600   **MAP LOCATION #18**
Kirkwood 63122   Stpeterkirkwood.org

After World War II St. Louis Catholics, like everyone else, found themselves in a changed world. Empty pews in the old city churches were signs of an exodus to the suburbs. A breeze was stirring that would in time bring major changes to the Church.

After more than a century of building churches that imitated the styles of medieval Europe, a new generation of American architects experimented with fresh approaches toward how a place of worship might look and feel. The simple lines, open spaces, and new materials of mid-century modernism offered cheerful places filled with natural light.

It's interesting that one of the region's oldest parishes would produce one of the earliest examples of modern design. St. Peter Church in Kirkwood became a parish in 1832, before the town even existed. After the Civil War, it built a church closer to the heart of downtown Kirkwood. In 1951, its forward-thinking pastor, Monsignor Alphonse Westhoff, led the effort to construct the current church.

St. Louis architect Joseph Murphy was developing a reputation as a creator of innovative, modern Catholic churches. His designs offered congregations fresh environments for prayer. Murphy incorporated the works of local artists such as Brother Mel Meyer and Rudolph Torrini into the new St. Peter. Parishioner and liturgical artist Francis Deck collaborated with Emil Frei & Associates to create a series of 24 tall, narrow stained glass windows which sweep like a wave of color and form across the eastern wall of the nave and into the sanctuary. Each window tells the story of some element of the Mass. The images along the wall of the nave represent the Liturgy of the Word. The windows that wrap around the sanctuary portray, in richer colors and patterns,

> But if we walk in the light, as He is in the light,
> we have fellowship with one another,
> and the blood of Jesus, his Son, purifies us from all sin.
>
> *1 John 1:7*

the Liturgy of the Eucharist. Above the sanctuary, a glass structure on the roof lets in natural light to fall upon the altar.

The Gothic, Romanesque, and Baroque churches of old mastered the art of creating prayerful moods through elaborate designs chiseled in stone. There are mysteries in the shadows. Their stained glass windows bring Scriptures to life in realistic detail. St. Peter in Kirkwood relies upon the abstract to free our imaginations. The spaces are open, fluid, and bright. The sun brings light and color through its windows, and the sense of joy that comes with illumination.

Stained glass windows wrap around the sanctuary, interpreting Scripture in modern, abstract images.

Side altar to Mary at St. Peter Church in downtown St. Charles.

St. Peter Catholic Church

St. Charles

221 First Capitol Dr.
St. Charles 63301

636.946.6641
Stpstc.org

MAP LOCATION #19

The cornerstone for St. Peter Church was laid in 1861 to replace the original wood structure which had served its German-speaking congregation for over a decade. Upon completion it was one of the largest Catholic churches west of the Mississippi River. Over the years it's undergone a series of expansions and enhancements as it assumed its place among St. Charles's many remarkable historical buildings.

The church is filled with liturgical art pieces from its long history. During a major expansion in 1910 the high altar, crafted in 1887, was restored and moved into the enlarged, new sanctuary, where it resides today. Other works include wooden statues, hand-carved in the 1860s, of several saints, and magnificent stained glass windows depicting the four Evangelists in their symbolic forms of angel, lion, ox, and eagle.

It's a place where history, art, and faith have shared a common space over the course of many generations.

> When they had finished breakfast, Jesus said to Simon Peter,
> "Simon, son of John, do you love me more than these?"
> He said to him, "Yes, Lord, you know that I love you."
> He said to him, "Feed my lambs."
>
> He then said to him a second time, "Simon, son of John, do you love me?"
> He said to him, "Yes, Lord, you know that I love you."
> He said to him, "Tend my sheep."
>
> He said to him the third time, "Simon, son of John, do you love me?"
> Peter was distressed that he had said to him a third time, "Do you love me?"
> and he said to him, "Lord, you know everything; you know that I love you."
> Jesus said to him, "Feed my sheep."
>
> *John 21:15–17*

One of 12 small oratories along the walls of the St. Vincent de Paul Chapel.

St. Vincent de Paul Chapel at Rigali Center

Shrewsbury

20 Archbishop May Dr.   314.792.7000   MAP LOCATION #20
Shrewsbury 63119

The atmosphere within the St. Vincent de Paul Chapel transports visitors to the late Middle Ages. Choir stalls and pews made of dark oak face each other across the main aisle. Above the high altar, stained glass windows bathe the sanctuary in soft, colored light. Elaborately carved screens frame a giant archway opening into the nave, while Gothic columns rise to support a barrel-arched ceiling. Twelve small oratories line the chapel's walls, each with its own altar and image of an apostle. A population of saints, carved in wood and stone, keep watch over the space from every possible angle.

The chapel holds a special place in the history of the St. Louis Archdiocese. It adjoins the lobby of the Cardinal Rigali Center, which was built in 1913 to house Kenrick Seminary. Since then, generations of young priests-in-training have said their prayers there. The seminary relocated in the 1980s, but the chapel remains a peaceful and beautiful place where visitors are welcome.

It was St. Vincent de Paul who founded the order that established the first seminary in Missouri in 1818 at St. Mary of the Barrens in Perryville. Naming the chapel after him honors the important role the Vincentians have played in seminary education for the past two centuries.

> St. Vincent, patron of all charitable associations
> and father of those who are in misery,
> come to our assistance.
>
> Obtain from our Lord help for the poor, relief for the infirm,
> consolation for the afflicted, protection for the abandoned,
> a spirit of generosity for the rich, grace of conversion for sinners,
> zeal for priests, peace for the church, tranquility and order for all nations,
> and salvation for them all.
>
> May we be united in the life to come, by your intercession,
> and experience joy, gladness, and everlasting happiness.

Grottos

A grotto is a small cave. Some are natural formations, but most religious grottos are of human design. They typically house a statue of the Virgin Mary, and as you visit holy sites throughout Missouri, you'll see quite a few of them in cemeteries and church gardens, on the grounds of the larger shrines and sometimes off by themselves.

First-century Christians were familiar with grottos erected around the idols of various Greek and Roman gods. As the Roman Empire became Christianized, many were incorporated into churches. The concept of the grotto as a place to visit and pray captured Catholic imaginations around the world when, in 1858, 14-year-old Bernadette Soubirous saw a lady dressed in white standing in a cave near the French town of Lourdes. In a series of apparitions, she revealed herself to Bernadette as the Virgin Mary. A spring began to flow from the cave, and its waters were credited with miraculous healing powers.

Throughout Missouri, pilgrims visit recreations of Bernadette praying before the Holy Mother, who stands before a cave and a pool of water. In many cases they are replenished by water brought in from Lourdes. The grottos combine elements of the artistic and the spiritual. The bright beauty of the Virgin emerges from the dark roughness of the stones. The presence of water reminds us of life—on earth and beyond. It was, we might even recall, at the mouth of a cave where the prophet Elijah himself experienced God.

Grotto of Our Lady of Lourdes at Mercy Conference and Retreat Center in St. Louis County.

At Visions of Peace, the atmosphere is conducive to solitude and prayer.

Come to me, all you who labor and are burdened, and I will give you rest.

Matthew 11:28

Visions of Peace

Pevely

1000 Abbey Ln.
Pevely 63070

636.475.3697
Vophermitages.org

MAP LOCATION #21

You'll get more out of your visit to Visions of Peace if you have an idea of what you're seeking there. Regardless of your faith, you're welcome to stay in one of their small hermitages along a bluff overlooking the Mississippi River. You may stay a few days or longer. You'll come by yourself. It's not designed for groups. You may choose to be left alone or receive some guidance from a spiritual mentor. At the beginning of your stay, you're likely to be blessed with a personal prayer, specific to your quest.

If that sounds a bit intimidating, it's because most of us are unaccustomed to solitude and stillness. We spend our time being productive, making deadlines, and reaching goals. We're busy people, quite at home in a state of mind and a way of life that protects us from thoughts of who we are, where we belong, and what it all means.

In 1974, Sister Miriam Clare Stoll of the Sisters of Providence of Saint Mary-of-the-Woods was inspired to create a place of prayer offering small, humble hermitages for visitors. She gathered support among her religious colleagues, and three years later a family donated a summer home on the river bluff near Pevely. Over the years several simple dwellings, a spirituality center, and a chapel have been built on the grounds. A separate hermitage offers a place for priests to stay and minister to those who ask for spiritual guidance.

Visions of Peace is a place where visitors, surrounded by the beauty of nature, may be so freed from the normal distractions of life, that they find the peace they need to discern God's will.

Several small hermitages with basic accommodations are built into a bluff overlooking the river.

White House Jesuit Retreat

Oakville

7400 Christopher Dr.   314.416.6400/800.643.1003   **MAP LOCATION #22**
Oakville 63129   Whretreat.org

Perched atop a bluff overlooking the Mississippi River, about 30 miles south of the Gateway Arch, is the campus of the White House Jesuit Retreat. In 1922, the Jesuits bought the old White House Farm to build an 80-acre getaway. Sweeping views of the river, winding paths through hills and woods, stunning sunrises and sunsets, and starry nights offer ideal places for contemplation and meditation.

A path running across the edge of the bluff leads visitors through an elaborately constructed Way of the Cross. Adjoining a small chapel at the top of the hill is a small anteroom replicating the cave in Manresa, Spain, where, 500 years ago, Jesuit founder Ignatius of Loyola was inspired to create his spiritual exercises. White House seems a world away, a place where the mind and heart break free from the routines of daily life and open to the bigger questions of how we get right with God.

Men and women of all faiths (even little faith) are welcome to participate in three-day silent retreats. Retreatants participate in a condensed version of Loyola's spiritual exercises, designed to free them from their own wills so they may more easily discern God's plan for them. And even if at the end of the retreat God's plan is still not

perfectly clear, the experience of not hearing one's own voice for the better part of three days can be liberating in its own way.

The grounds are closed during retreats, but visitors are free to wander them on Sundays from 3 p.m. to dusk or by appointment.

Chapel, where daily Mass and talks are held for retreatants.

Silence and the spiritual exercises of St. Ignatius of Loyola are practiced by visitors of the White House Jesuit Retreat.
Photo, Larry Hassel.

Lord Jesus, teach me to be generous.
Teach me to serve You as you deserve;
to give and not to count the cost,
to fight and not to heed the wounds,
to toil and not to seek for rest,
to labor and not to ask for reward,
save that of knowing that I will do Your will.

St. Ignatius Loyola

Imaginative Prayer

The human imagination is a gift that can transport us beyond the limits of the physical world. It lets us visualize the miraculous and bolster our faith in matters that defy practical experience. If we are truly created in the image of God, then our tiny imaginations might even be sparks of the Divine. This is powerful stuff, trusting our hearts to venture where the head can't go. If there's a way to apply it to prayer, there's no telling what might happen.

This is where St. Ignatius Loyola enters the picture. The 16th-century founder of the Jesuits discovered a way to meditate on Scripture that draws upon the power of imagination to engage us more closely with Jesus Christ. Unlike most typical forms of Bible study, Ignatian meditation asks us to imagine as we read a Gospel passage that we are within the scene, witnessing it as it unfolds. It's a kind of prayer that encourages us to bring our senses fully into the process as we imagine the colors, sounds, smells, and tastes that make reading the Gospel more than an intellectual experience. Can you see the crowd? What are they wearing? Are there animals? Is someone baking bread? Imagine that you are in the presence of a physical Jesus. What does he look like? Can you imagine his voice? His eyes? What would you say to him if you had the chance? How would that feel?

Ignatian contemplation deserves more than a brief description, and it's important to understand that it's not a renunciation of thoughtful analysis and deductive thinking. But for those who pursue it seriously, it can be a powerful means of letting God talk to us through the gates of imagination.

Statue of St. Ignatius Loyola on the campus of Saint Louis University in St. Louis.

More than ever I find myself in the hands of God.
This is what I have wanted all my life from my youth.

But now there is a difference;
the initiative is entirely with God.

It is indeed a profound spiritual experience
to know and feel myself so totally in God's hands.

Pedro Arrupe, SJ

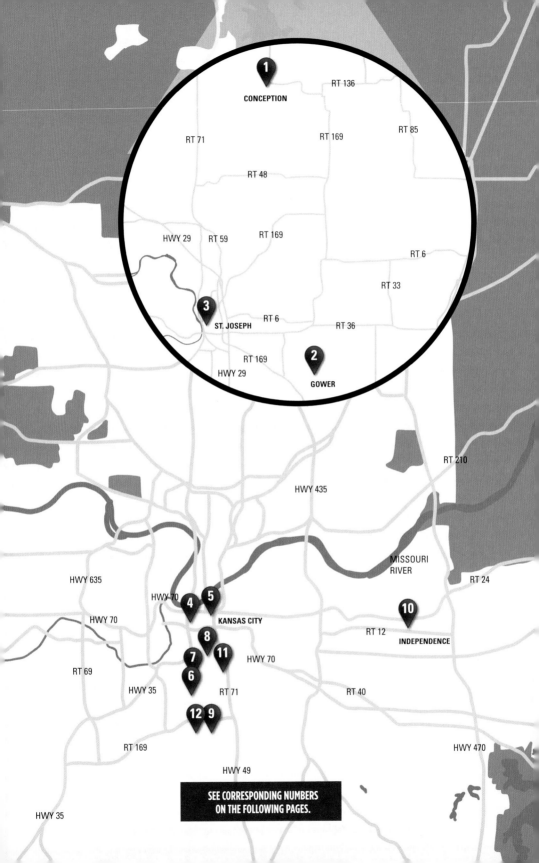

SEE CORRESPONDING NUMBERS
ON THE FOLLOWING PAGES.

11

Diocese of Kansas City— St. Joseph

The Basilica of the Immaculate Conception conveys a simple and unpretentious beauty.

Basilica of the Immaculate Conception

Conception

37174 State Hwy. VV Conception 64433	660.944.3100 Conceptionabbey.org	**MAP LOCATION #1**

When Father Frowin Conrad arrived with a small band of monks to this remote spot in northern Missouri in 1873, he brought with him the vision of a community based on St. Benedict's principles for a balanced life of work and prayer. The monks served the region's Irish and German settlers, establishing a tradition of working as pastors, chaplains, teachers, and artisans that continues today.

When it came time to build a church, Abbot Frowin insisted on a structure that would in every sense serve as the heart of Conception Abbey. Everything about it must be solid, simple, and graceful. In his Swiss homeland, monasteries were typically built in the elaborate style of the Baroque. The abbot favored Romanesque, sturdy and unpretentious, and less likely to distract worshippers from their focus on God.

The interior maintains that same simplicity with a dignified elegance. A key feature is a collection of frescoes along the upper walls. The style is called Beuronese, after the monastery in southern Germany where it was created. In the 1890s, its muted colors and simple lines were considered revolutionary. When the monks at Immaculate Conception learned that no artists from Beuron were available to paint the murals, they took on the job themselves, creating replicas of paintings from other monasteries. Twelve murals on the walls of the nave depict scenes from the lives of Jesus and Mary. Four in the transepts represent the lives of St. Benedictine and his sister St. Scholastica. In the apse, high above the altar, a painting of the Immaculate Conception depicts Mary as the new Eve, triumphing over evil.

From a distance, the view of the basilica, surrounded by fields, could be a scene from medieval times. It might have been in the mind of Abbot Frowin when he said, "Now there stands a temple in which the all-highest God might receive the honor due Him and the people their needed blessings."

Benedictines of Mary, Queen of Apostles

Gower

8005 NW 316th St.
Gower 64454   Benedictinesofmary.org

MAP LOCATION #2

Jesus, in his last moments on the Cross, asked the beloved disciple John and his mother Mary to accept each other as mother and son. Catholic tradition holds that Mary lived her last days at John's home in Ephesus, offering her spiritual support to the young Church. The Benedictine Sisters of Mary in rural northwest Missouri emulate that tradition, dedicating themselves to supporting the Church and its priests.

St. Benedict's motto *Ora et Labora* (prayer and work) governs their lives. Throughout the day the sisters pray the Liturgy of the Hours in Latin. There's farm work, tending orchards and gardens, cows and chickens, dogs, bees, and cats. They craft priestly apparel and altar cloths, appreciated for their quality throughout the world. Each stitch in a vestment, they say, is a prayer for the priest who will wear it. They also create greeting and religious cards.

The sisters speak only when necessary. Silence makes it easier for them to hear God, who tends to speak softly. But from their daily prayers and songs, they've been inspired to produce several recordings of religious music that have earned top places on the *Billboard* charts. In 2013, they were the first nuns to win the magazine's award for "Classical Artist of the Year."

It's difficult for most people to understand cloistered life, cut off from the people and events of the outside world. But these women, with the humor and joy they bring to their days, clearly live in a world of fullness and completeness. They do their best to be for today's church what Mary was to the first Apostles, a source of encouragement, support, and prayer from a place of solitude.

> When Jesus saw his mother and the disciple there whom he loved, he said to his mother, "Woman, behold, your son." Then he said to the disciple, "Behold, your mother." And from that hour the disciple took her into his home.
>
> *John 19:26–27*

The Holy Mother welcomes prayers at the Cathedral of St. Joseph.

Cathedral of St. Joseph

St. Joseph

519 N 10th St.	816.232.7763	MAP LOCATION #3
St. Joseph 64501	Cathedralsj.org	

The city of St. Joseph grew from a fur trading post into a rough-and-tumble jumping-off point to the Wild West. It was a starting point for the Pony Express. Jesse James was murdered there. Visiting Jesuit missionaries did their best to tone things down, and in 1845, a young Irish priest by the name of Thomas Scanlan arrived and managed the construction of St. Joseph Church. In 1868, when the Vatican created the Diocese of St. Joseph, it became a cathedral. It was replaced by the current structure in 1873.

The cathedral has seen several renovations since then. The most recent was in 1995, in conjunction with its sesquicentennial. Many of the original features were restored and new design elements incorporated to enhance its beauty. One hundred fifty stars were painted on a blue, arched ceiling. Marble tiles were laid into the middle

aisle to match those in the sanctuary. It's a bright and open place. Two rows of ionic columns run the length of the nave, rising to meet gracefully designed arches beneath the starry sky. Tall, narrow windows illuminate this holy place that celebrates the Light of the World.

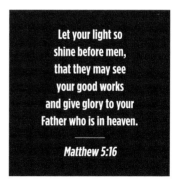

Let your light so shine before men, that they may see your good works and give glory to your Father who is in heaven.

Matthew 5:16

The sanctuary is bright and spacious.

Cathedral of the Immaculate Conception

Kansas City—Quality Hill

416 W 12th St.   816.842.0416   **MAP LOCATION #4**
Kansas City 64105   Kcgolddome.org

There's been a Catholic church on the same corner of Broadway since 1835. From log house to brick church to cathedral, it's been central to the city's Catholic heritage from its frontier days. Kansas City became its own diocese in 1880, and two years later construction began on its new cathedral. Ten thousand people attended the dedication of its cornerstone. Three thousand attended the first Mass a year later. Built on the highest point in the city, its copper dome could be seen easily from surrounding neighborhoods.

Over the years, other improvements would further secure its status as a city landmark. In 1895, a carillon of 11 bells was installed in the tower. Local artisans installed 16 handcrafted stained glass windows in 1912. Decades later, the dome and cupola were covered with 23-carat gold leaf. On sunny days it shines spectacularly. Illuminated at night, the effect is dramatic.

In 2003, an extensive renovation of the interior struck an artistic balance of the traditional and contemporary. Some call the result "modern neoclassical." The nave is lined on either side with fluted Corinthian columns supporting arches beneath a barrel-vaulted ceiling. The sanctuary is open, uncovered, and placed toward the center of the church with seating placed around it. The floor beneath the altar is slightly raised, curved, and hewn from stone that shines with a golden hue. Throughout the church, modern art lives comfortably with the architecture of the original church.

Art and design of different styles and from different eras are compatible when grounded in common faith. The mood they create at the Cathedral of the Immaculate Conception seems to bridge time and carry that faith forward.

Ancient and contemporary design combine to create "modern neoclassical" spaces at the Cathedral of the Immaculate Conception.

Daily Examen

We measure our time on earth in days, and a typical day for most of us plays out like a jumble of disconnected events accompanied by a blur of emotional flashes. We know that God is in there somewhere among the clutter, but we can't cut through the tangle to see the big plan.

This isn't a modern problem. Five hundred years ago, Ignatius of Loyola included in his Spiritual Exercises a technique he called the Daily Examen to help his Jesuit followers find God among the chaos. It consists of five basic steps.

First, find a quiet space, thank God for the gift of another day, and ask help from the Holy Spirit to make some sense out of it.

Next, review the day in detail. Where did you go? What did you do? Who did you meet? Let yourself be guided by a sense of gratitude. What small gifts and joys did you experience along the way? Are there actions you regret?

Then, shift your focus to how you responded emotionally to the events of your day. This is where things can get tangled. In a single 24-hour period, feelings might range from happiness, compassion, and enthusiasm to anger, envy, and frustration. Review them with God and look to see if they shine light on your path.

Get specific. Let the Holy Spirit guide you to a single moment of your day—an emotion, an event, an interaction with another person—and make it the center of a prayer. You might find yourself expressing thanks, asking for forgiveness, or requesting help for yourself or another.

Finally, look toward tomorrow in the light of what your examination has revealed. Ask for guidance, help, and hope.

The Examen isn't a time to beat yourself up over where you have fallen short. It's more of a friendly, open conversation with God in which you sort through the messy confusion of your day. It's an opportunity to consider the small, easily overlooked, but precious gifts that came your way. It's a chance to identify some areas for self-improvement. And it reserves some moments to reflect upon the miracle of having spent another day as a conscious part of God's creation.

The Daily Examen, a prayerful review of your day.
Photo, Tony Carosella.

May it please the supreme and divine Goodness
to give us all abundant grace
ever to know His most holy will
and perfectly to fulfill it.

St. Ignatius of Loyola

Old St. Patrick's Oratory

Kansas City—East Village

806 Cherry St.
Kansas City 64106

816.931.5612
Institute-christ-king.org/kansascity-home

MAP LOCATION #5

Guardian of Catholic traditions.

Old St. Patrick's Oratory is the oldest standing Catholic church in Kansas City. That it's survived a century and a half of urban growth gnawing at its doorstep is a minor miracle.

In the years following the Civil War, large numbers of Irish Catholics moved to Kansas City, attracted by the abundance of low-paying, dangerous jobs a young, booming city had to offer its unskilled workers. They paved the streets, laid the bricks, built the railroad, and put their coins in the offering plate on Sunday mornings. By the 1880s, Kansas City was the only place in the state where Irish immigrants outnumbered German.

They got their own parish in 1868 and celebrated their first Mass in what was then the new St. Patrick's on Christmas of 1875. It was a magnificent structure and a source of pride. But by the turn of the 20th century an expanding downtown was pushing its parishioners out of the surrounding neighborhoods. There was talk in the 1960s of tearing the church down to make way for a freeway. Its survival seemed unlikely.

In 2005, it became an Oratory under the direction of the Institute of Christ the King Sovereign Priest, a society dedicated to preserving the Latin Mass and other pre-Vatican II liturgical traditions. As an Oratory its membership was no longer restricted to a particular geographical area. An extensive renovation was completed in 2008, and today Old St. Patrick's is a local landmark, a monument to the city's Catholic past, and a guardian of its traditions.

Our Lady of Good Counsel Catholic Church

Kansas City—Westport

3934 Washington St.
Kansas City 64111

816.561.0400
Goodcounselkc.org

MAP LOCATION #6

On Thanksgiving Day in 1907, Our Lady of Good Counsel opened its doors to the growing numbers of immigrants, mostly Irish, moving into the city's Westport area. It was built in a style called Palladianism, often seen in old Irish churches, that favors classical symmetry and simplicity.

The altar was made in Italy of Carrara marble, a favorite among sculptors since ancient Rome. The windows along the side walls portray the Joyful Mysteries and key moments from the life of Christ in a rich palette of colors.

Altar with Image of Divine Mercy.

Our Lady of Good Counsel is the Diocesan shrine of the Divine Mercy. The Image of Divine Mercy, inspired by the visions of the Polish nun Sr. Faustina Kowalska, sits above the main altar. After every Mass the Chaplet of the Divine Mercy is recited, promising to all the certainty of Christ's grace and mercy.

> **"I am love and Mercy Itself.**
> **There is no misery that could be a match for My mercy,**
> **neither will misery exhaust it,**
> **because as it is being granted—it increases.**
> **The soul that trusts in My mercy is most fortunate,**
> **because I Myself take care of it."**
>
> *Jesus's words to Sr. Faustina, as recorded in her diary.*

Visitors of Our Lady of Perpetual Help enter a place of awesome, Old World grandeur.

Our Lady of Perpetual Help Catholic Church

Kansas City—Westport

3333 Broadway Blvd.   816.561.3771   MAP LOCATION #7
Kansas City 64111   Redemptoristkc.org

Kansas City grew rapidly in the decade following the Civil War. Immigrants from Ireland, Germany, Italy, Southern Europe, and Latin America weaved their Catholic traditions into the social fabric of the city. In 1876, the Redemptorist Fathers built a monastery in the nearby town of Westport and welcomed local families to the chapel they dedicated to Our Lady of Perpetual Help.

Westport eventually became part of the city, a church replaced the chapel, and the working-class families, many from the city's Kerry Patch neighborhood, worked their way into the American middle class. When the Redemptorists broke ground for a grand, French Gothic church on Broadway in 1907, 15,000 people attended, and a stream of processions celebrated the city's ethnic cultures as the church's foundation. At its dedication four years later, the local press hailed Our Lady of Perpetual Help as a major architectural achievement.

Its heavy limestone exterior is brightened by Gothic details, lending an impressive presence to one of Kansas City's main thoroughfares. The interior features, among its many treasures, five altars crafted from white Italian marble, mosaic Stations of the Cross, and blue-tinted stained glass windows.

This church, built around an icon in which a mother comforts her son, brings a sense of peace to those who visit. Art and design combine to create an atmosphere of quiet solitude and beauty. It's a place that sets our minds to rest and where prayers come easily.

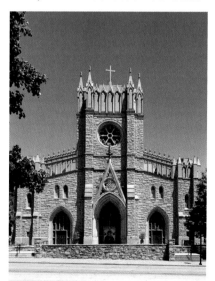

French Gothic on Broadway.

Stations of the Cross

Pilgrimages have played an important part in Christian devotion since the earliest days of the Church. Sacred journeys serve as metaphors for our lives on earth and have the power to energize us spiritually. The effort they require strengthens our spiritual commitment. They offer adventure and escape from the routines of daily life, sharpening our senses and opening us to fresh insights. The Stations of the Cross require less than a full-blown trek to the Holy Land, but they get us off our knees and set us off on a mini-pilgrimage through Christ's last day on earth as a man.

Whether the stations themselves are small plaques on a church wall or statues along a winding garden path, each portrays one of 14 moments of the Passion, from Jesus's condemnation by Pilate to his placement in the tomb. Some of the scenes are described in the Gospels; others have grown out of tradition. The faithful stop at each image to say prayers and reflect, particularly during Lent and on Good Friday.

The Stations of the Cross offer us a way to pray that keeps us focused as we walk, stop, reflect, and shift gears through a series of images and events that lead us to the primary reason for Christ's time on earth.

It's often noted that there should be one more station, representing the empty tomb and the resurrected Christ. But there's nothing to keep us from offering our own prayer at the end of the pilgrimage to give thanks for that miracle and make our journey complete.

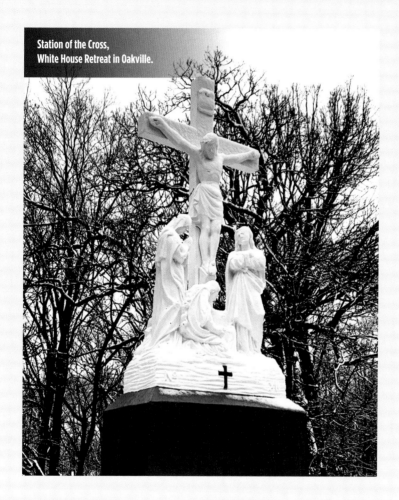

Station of the Cross,
White House Retreat in Oakville.

My Lord Jesus Christ, you have made this journey to die for me with infinite love.
So many times I have sinned, but I repent sincerely because I love you.
Pardon me, my God. I will love you all my life.

Opening Prayer, Stations of the Cross

Our Lady of Sorrows Catholic Church

Kansas City—Crown Center

| 2552 Gillham Rd. | 816.421.2112 | **MAP LOCATION #8** |
| Kansas City 64108 | Oloskc.org | |

When plans for Kansas City's new Union Station called for construction on the site of a church, Our Lady of Sorrows packed up and moved. That was in 1906, and reports of the day describe how the German American parishioners carted its furnishings, statues, and art up the hill to their new church. The congregation grew steadily, and in 1923, they replaced it with the present church, praised at its dedication as a magnificent architectural achievement.

The interior is gracefully shaped by arches and columns. Its art glass windows present designs and symbols from Christian faith—a heart, an anchor, crown, or cross—rather than scenes from Scriptures. Colors are purposely used to lend emotional dimensions to the glass: purple for sorrow; green for hope; yellow, joy.

Above the altar, winged angels extend their arms upward to support a large golden crown. According to local lore, parishioner Joyce C. Hall

was inspired one Sunday to make a crown the logo of his company, Hallmark Cards.

The sorrowful Mary, *Mater Dolorosa*, is a theme that runs throughout Catholic devotion. Upon the altar of this church, she stands beside her crucified son, hands clasped to her heart and head bowed, bearing her sorrow with strength and dignity.

Graceful design and bright colors bring cheer to a place named for sorrow.

St. Thérèse de Lisieux stands before the altar of Our Lady of Sorrows, where angels hold high a golden crown.

St. Francis Xavier Church was honored by
the American Institute of Architects for design excellence.
Photo, St. Francis Xavier Catholic Church.

St. Francis Xavier Catholic Church

Kansas City—Western 49-63 Neighborhood

1001 E 52nd St.
Kansas City 64110

816.523.5115
Sfx-kc.org

MAP LOCATION #9

When St. Francis Xavier opened in 1950, it created quite a stir. Pastor John Gerst, SJ put it tactfully: "The beauty and nobility of the edifice will grow on you, I know." But it took a while for the church to achieve widespread acceptance as an architectural marvel.

It's not surprising that the Jesuits, with their open-minded tendencies, would be the instigators of such a progressive building. They hired Barry Byrne, a protegee of Frank Lloyd Wright, to create a church that would break from centuries-old designs and serve as a model for a new generation of church architects.

Byrne, with the assistance of Joseph Shaughnessy, designed the church in the shape of an oval, juxtaposing curves and straight vertical lines for a dynamic, completely unconventional shape. Modern materials like concrete and tiles on the exterior speak to an age of new technologies. Aluminum accents along the porch are matched in the altar ornaments.

A low-ceilinged narthex opens into a spacious interior, introducing an element of surprise to a first-time visitor. Tall, narrow windows, tint-ed blue, let in soft, natural light. The focus of attention is the red-and

rust-colored sanctuary with its large gold and silver Christ, created by sculptor Alfonso Iannelli.

This church is extraordinary not just because it breaks with tradition or has the capacity to shock or surprise. What's refreshing about it is how it shows us Christianity still has the power to inspire new and creative ideas to express faith, and how closely linked are belief and imagination.

A fresh approach to church design.
Photo, Peter F. Malone.

St. Mary's Catholic Church

Independence

600 N Liberty St.
Independence 64050

816.252.0121
Saintmarysparish.org

MAP LOCATION #10

Named for the nation's founding document, the city of Independence has seen its share of historic events. Mormon founder Joseph Smith predicted the Second Coming of Christ would occur there. It was the starting point for the California, Oregon, and Santa Fe trails and, along with the town of St. Joseph, a launching station for the Pony Express. It witnessed two Civil War battles. Harry and Bess Truman called it home.

Since 1823, Independence has also been the home of St. Mary's, the oldest parish in the Diocese of Kansas City-St. Joseph. So, it's not surprising that a parish that's seen two centuries of colorful history would choose to be colorful in its own way. Since the current church opened its doors in 1865 it's undergone several renovations, but in celebration of its 150th birthday, parishioners took remodeling in a new direction, working with an art studio to develop a new and unusual, but essentially Catholic, aesthetic.

Parishioners worked side by side with artists, designers, and construction workers to recreate the sanctuary. The creative team

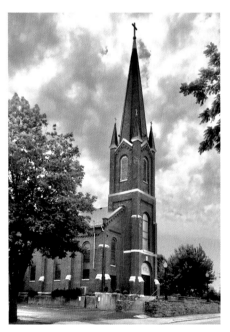

painted murals and decorative designs on the walls from floor to ceiling. Mosaic patterns adorn a new altar, lectern, ambo, and tabernacle. During the process workers found the original Stations of the Cross and reinstalled them.

The changes have transformed this historic church into a visual delight, employing art to reinvigorate the traditional while bringing attention to the essential beauty of the Catholic faith.

St. Mary's in Independence.

St. Mary's—contemporary, colorful, and Catholic.

SANCTUS ✦ SANCTUS ✦ SANCTUS

Recent restoration has brought St. Vincent de Paul
back to its original beauty.

Do not overburden yourself with rules of devotion,
but persist in doing well those you have:
your daily actions, your work;
in a word, let everything revolve around doing well
what you are doing.

St. Vincent de Paul

St. Vincent de Paul Catholic Church

Kansas City—Midtown

3106 Flora Ave.   816.923.0202   **MAP LOCATION #11**
Kansas City 64109   Stvincentkc.org

When renowned architect Maurice Carroll designed what he called "a true Gothic parish church," he received the American Institute of Architects' medal for church design. Unlike the traditional European Gothic cathedrals with their elaborate ornamentation, this was a simpler version of the style, appropriate for a parish and designed so that the congregation's attention would be focused on the altar. Completed in 1924, it was a 16th-century building quite at home in a 20th-century city.

Despite its elegance, the church fell on hard times, and in 1970 the diocese closed it. Ten years later the Society of Saint Pius X bought and reopened it as a church where they could offer their brand of conservative Catholicism to Roman Catholics who felt left behind by changes in the Church.

The Society is a fraternity of Catholic priests which rejects most of the reforms of Vatican II. It was founded in 1970 by the late French Archbishop Marcel Lefebvre, a controversial figure in the Church and a leader of the movement to restore the traditional Latin Mass and return to pre-Vatican II practices. In 2016, the Society launched a three-year,

multimillion-dollar renovation that restored the original beauty of the building.

Since the Church's earliest days, it's struggled with issues regarding tradition and reform. It's possible that these debates are of more interest to us than they are to God. St. Vincent de Paul is a beautiful place to visit, an architectural and artistic expression of Catholic faith.

A Gothic presence in Midtown Kansas City.

Our Lady of Guadalupe

Debates over the existence of miracles rarely change minds. Those who believe in them understand the universe as a place where spiritual and physical dimensions coexist and sometimes overlap. Skeptics put their faith more readily in what they can weigh and measure. So, we have science to understand the physical, and faith to grasp the spiritual, each bringing its own set of tools to our task of understanding the big picture. From time to time incidents occur that defy everything reason and common sense lead us to expect. The most rational among us point to possible causes, like rare astronomical phenomena, mass hypnosis, optical illusions, or hallucination. Others simply believe that a miracle occurred.

There was such an incident on a hill outside Mexico City in December of 1531. A farmer by the name of Juan Diego experienced a series of apparitions in which a young woman described herself as the "mother of the very true deity." She asked that a church be built on the site in her honor. Diego had no luck convincing the archbishop. The mysterious woman had a plan: Diego was to gather flowers, which appeared on the barren, winter hillside. She arranged them in his *tilma*, or cloak, and sent him back to the archbishop. When he opened the garment, the flowers fell to the floor, revealing on the fabric an image of a woman, standing in prayer upon a crescent moon, surrounded by a burst of golden rays.

Today, Juan Diego's *tilma* is displayed at the Basilica of Our Lady of Guadalupe in Mexico City, the most-visited Catholic shrine in the world. It has become a symbol for Mexican Catholicism and national pride. Adopted by the pro-life movement, it appears in Catholic churches around the world.

For a 500-year-old coat, it is uncannily well-preserved. Evidence suggests some minor artistic embellishments over the years, but the source or method of its creation has not been scientifically determined. After centuries of legends, examinations, and scholarly hypotheses, it remains for millions an article of faith.

The image of Our Lady of Guadalupe, preserved in the cloak of Juan Diego for 500 years.

Visitation of the Blessed Virgin Mary is rich in the beauty and charm of the missions of the Southwest.

Visitation of the Blessed Virgin Mary Catholic Church

Kansas City—Countryside

5141 Main St. 816.753.7422 MAP LOCATION #12
Kansas City 64112 Visitation.org

American architects at the turn of the 20th century were rediscovering the charm of old Spanish missions. Across the country, buildings ranging from movie theaters and auto showrooms to new homes were springing up in the shapes, colors, and textures of the Southwest. When Visitation parish constructed its new church in 1915, they modeled it after the 18th-century Old Mission in Santa Barbara. Local lore has it that the church inspired the developer of Country Club Plaza to adopt a similar design for his 1920s shopping center.

In time, a growing congregation required more space. In 2004, the parish took on the challenge of preserving the appeal of its original design while enlarging and updating the old building. On the outside, the ochre-colored stucco walls, arched walkways, and red tiled roof remain unchanged. Inside, visitors pass through a spacious narthex with the unmistakable flavor of colonial Spain before entering a large and open nave. Pews fan around the altar on three sides, contributing to a sense of shared community. Carved wooden statues of saints and angels occupy places throughout the church. The walls are decorated with designs painted in pale and subtle colors. Three adjoining, smaller chapels are open for prayer and Mass. All incorporate the materials and craftsmanship of Mexico and the American Southwest.

Catholic churches come in a variety of styles, grown from the cultures of its people living in different places and times. Gothic and Romanesque amaze us with designs that seem to exist beyond time. Mid-century modern plays with light, space, and the abstract to clear our senses and help us adjust our focus. Visitation of the Blessed Virgin Mary offers visitors a feeling for the rich Catholic traditions to our south.

RT 15

RT 6

ST. PATRICK
RT 61
RT 81

MISSISSIPPI
RIVER

RT 156

RT 63

RT 61

RT 41

RT 36
RT 61

RT 87

INDIAN CREEK
RT 24

BRUSH CREEK

HWY 70

CENTER

RT 65

RT 87

RT 23

SEDALIA

RT 5

RT 50

RT 19

RT 52

RT 161

HWY 70

MISSOURI
RIVER

RT 54

RT 94
STARKENBURG

HERMANN

JEFFERSON CITY

BONNOTS MILL
FRANKENSTEIN

RT 19

RT 50

RT 50

RT 135

RT 54

RT 5
RT 52

RT 135

LAURIE

**SEE CORRESPONDING NUMBERS
ON THE FOLLOWING PAGES.**

Diocese of
Jefferson City

Cathedral of St. Joseph

Jefferson City

2305 W Main St. 573.635.7991 **MAP LOCATION #1**
Jefferson City 65109 Cathedral.diojeffcity.org

The Cathedral of St. Joseph was designed in the heady days of Vatican II. When it opened in 1968, it replaced the old St. Peter's as the Mother Church of the Jefferson City Diocese. Many Catholics had never seen anything quite like it. It was circular and open, embodying the new spirit of inclusion. The architecture was bold, inviting visitors to approach their faith with renewed wonder.

But even the modern can show its age, and a major update was completed in 2023. A guiding idea behind the renovation was to use the power of art to bring worshippers into communion with God. A blend of traditional and contemporary design reminds visitors that faith isn't tied to a single period of history or style or taste.

A new outdoor canopy and a set of bell towers enhance the exterior. The interior space is still circular, but the sanctuary has a new crucifix, altar, ambo, and bishop's chair. Artists from across Missouri and Europe have created sculpture, mosaics, and paintings to adorn special places for prayer throughout the cathedral, including shrines to the Sacred Heart of Jesus, Our Lady of Guadalupe, and St. Rose Philippine Duchesne. New stained glass windows depict scenes from the Old and New Testaments and the lives of saints.

It's possible to respect tradition while being open to new ways of building and sharing our faith. The Cathedral of St. Joseph welcomes believers in a modern world to a place that is contemporary and yet unmistakably Roman Catholic.

The Cathedral before renovation.
Photo, Jay Nies.

Drawing of the Cathedral's new sanctuary.
William Heyer Architect.©

Angels flank the walls on either side of Immaculate Conception's sanctuary, rejoicing as Jesus becomes present on the altar.

Immaculate Conception Catholic Church

Jefferson City

1206 E McCarty St.   573.635.6143   **MAP LOCATION #2**
Jefferson City 65101   Icangels.com

For years, most Catholics in Jefferson City attended the old St. Peter Church beside the state capitol, but in time their growing numbers called for a second parish. A simple, brick church was constructed in 1913. Ten years later, the present Immaculate Conception Church opened on McCarty Street, a major thoroughfare at the time.

The doctrine of the Immaculate Conception teaches that Mary, the Mother of God, was conceived without sin. Immaculate Conception Church employs art and design in a variety of creative ways to honor the Holy Mother and place her within the story of her son's work on earth.

The architecture imparts a sense of a place where Heaven is not far away. The broad, vaulted ceiling is a canopy arching above worshippers, while gold and silver stars painted on the ceiling of the sanctuary create a celestial sky above the altar.

In the transept, a stained glass window depicts Jesus, the Good Shepherd, protecting His sheep. Another portrays the Blessed Mother as she is described in the Book of Revelation, clothed in the sun with the moon at her feet. Windows in the nave refer to the Rosary. Those on the left represent the Joyful Mysteries; on the right, the Glorious.

Smaller and less conspicuous decorative elements pay further tribute to Mary. Her image is on medallions in the ceiling, and the *fleur-de-lis*, a symbol of the Trinity and of nobility (such as a queen), appears in various places throughout the church.

It is a special place, devoted to appreciation of a mother's love.

"Christ of the Highway,"
blessing traffic on McCarty Street.

The Rosary

The Holy Rosary has evolved over the past thousand years as a venerated aid to prayer. Rosaries range from simple, knotted pieces of string to precious heirlooms and works of art. They have become a cherished part of Catholic tradition, because they offer a structured guide to ancient prayers and the remembrance of Holy Mysteries. The Rosary may be prayed in solitary silence or as part of a group. If you find you're a little shaky on the exact order of the prayers or the words, there's no shame in refreshing your memory with some help from Google.

There is a joyful physical aspect to praying the Rosary. The tactile sensation of our fingers as they move from bead to bead keeps us grounded, while the repetition of Hail Marys puts us in a meditative state of mind.

Finding the right words to address God is not always easy. The Rosary relieves us of that burden, guiding us through a landscape of prayers in which we reaffirm our faith, visit moments from Christ's life on earth, and contemplate the virtues of his mother.

Guide to prayers and mysteries.

Hail Mary, full of grace,
the Lord is with thee.
Blessed art thou among women,
and blessed is the fruit of thy womb, Jesus.

Holy Mary, Mother of God,
pray for us sinners
now and at the hour of our death.

National Shrine of Mary, Mother of the Church

Laurie

176 Marian Dr.	573.374.6279	**MAP LOCATION #3**
Laurie 65037		
Thenationalshrineofmarymotherofthechurch.com		

When Bagnell Dam opened in 1931, a large region of farmland in central Missouri was quickly transformed into the state's outdoor playground. Small towns finding themselves close to the 1,200 miles of new lakeshore were forever changed by a tourist and real estate boom.

The dominant religions in that part of the state are Evangelical and Protestant. In the 1980s, the small Catholic church of St. Patrick in Laurie, noticing an increasing number of Catholic tourists attending its Masses, built outdoor amphitheater and shrine to Mary. Following its dedication in 1988, it's become a destination for visitors from around the world.

The center of the shrine is a 14-foot, stainless steel statue of Mary, depicted as a young and energetic woman. And though the shrine is dedicated to the mother of Jesus, it's a tribute to all mothers. The names of thousands of women of all faiths are honored on the shrine's Mothers' Wall, a polished, black granite memorial to mothers and those who have served nurturing roles in the lives of others.

A small lake sits beside the amphitheater. A path leads through a wooded area past Stations of the Cross. The adjoining St. Patrick Church is modern and bright, with large glass windows providing views of the Ozark countryside.

God's love is vast, eternal, and beyond our total comprehension. A mother's love speaks directly to our hearts. That is worthy of a shrine.

> **Mother, help our faith!**
> Open our ears to hear God's word and to recognize His voice and call.
> Awaken in us a desire to follow in His footsteps,
> to go forth from our own land and to receive his promise.
>
> *Pope Francis*

Our Lady Help of Christians Catholic Church

Frankenstein

1665 Hwy. C
Frankenstein 65016

573.897.2587

MAP LOCATION #4

Clustered in an area of farmland southeast of Jefferson City are several small towns, each with its own historic Catholic church. There's St. Joseph in Westphalia, St. Francis Xavier in Taos, Immaculate Conception in Loose Creek, and others, connected by two-lane roads that wind and dip and hug the hillsides. The first sign that a town lies ahead is often the profile of a steeple rising from the landscape.

One of those little towns is Frankenstein, Missouri, and, yes, the residents have heard all the jokes. There are competing stories about how the town got its name, but none of them has anything to do with Mary Shelley's monster. Our Lady Help of Christians is without doubt the town's most imposing structure. Constructed of locally quarried stone and built in the Romanesque style, it looks as if it could have been standing there on Highway C since the Middle Ages.

Frankenstein has an interesting history, because unlike most Missouri settlements, the parish predates the town. In the 1860s, Jesuit priests established mission churches for the nearby farmers, most of whom had immigrated from the Rhineland. In the 1890s, the parish priest, Father John Bachmeier, led an effort to create a town for his church. In 1922, the parish built Our Lady Help of Christians, where it stands today in the heart of the village.

> **Most Holy Virgin Mary, Help of Christians,**
> **how sweet it is to come to your feet imploring your perpetual help.**
>
> **If earthly mothers cease not to remember their children,**
> **how can you, the most loving of all mothers, forget me?**
>
> *From a prayer by St. John Bosco*

Sacred Heart Chapel

Sedalia

421 W 3rd St.   660.827.2311   **MAP LOCATION #5**
Sedalia 65361   Svdpparish.diojeffcity.org

Sedalia's history has a touch of the Old West. A former railroad town, it was once the destination for massive cattle drives, attracting cowboys and others prone to mischief. Scott Joplin created his outrageous musical genre of ragtime there. Prostitution grew into a major industry. In 1877, the *St. Louis Post-Dispatch* declared the town "the Sodom and Gomorrah of the 19th century."

Today it's better known as home to the State Fair and a major stop along the cross-state Katy bike trail. The vintage architecture of its downtown and centrally located courthouse grounds give it the feel of a Hollywood movie set.

Sacred Heart Chapel, along with St. John the Evangelist and St. Patrick, are three historic churches in the parish of St. Vincent de Paul. Sacred Heart opened in 1882, and the twin spires of the current church have been a local landmark since 1894.

German congregations of the day loved their Gothic arches. Sacred Heart has its share both inside and out, inspiring thoughts of a kingdom beyond the clouds. The original, hand-carved altar offers niches for a range of saints including the Jesuits' St. Francis Xavier, German apostle St. Boniface, and St. Thérèse of Lisieux, who clutches

the flowers she promises to rain down upon us from Heaven. Altars to Mary and Joseph stand in their places beside the main altar, hosting even more saints. St. Patrick himself has claimed a place to display his Irish shamrock in this very German church.

We are thankful for whatever role Sacred Heart might have played in taming this once-rowdy town and putting Sedalia into God's good graces.

Bringing civility to the Wild West.

Shrine of Our Lady of Sorrows

Starkenburg

197 State Hwy. P
Starkenburg 65069

855.781.4824
Historicshrine.com

MAP LOCATION #6

The many sufferings of the Holy Mother have been a focus of Catholic devotion for more than 800 years. The intent has never been to portray a morose or self-pitying Mary, but to share her distress through our own disappointments and pain.

The story of the Shrine of Our Lady of Sorrows begins with the troubles of the people of Starkenburg, Missouri, in 1891. Threatened by torrential rains, they vowed to conduct an annual pilgrimage in honor of Our Lady of Sorrows if the storms would stop. They did, and the tradition continues today.

The grounds of the shrine are tucked in among the hills of Missouri's river country. Patches of forest dot the countryside, and cattle low in an adjoining field. It's easy to see how the region reminded settlers arriving in the 1840s of their home in Germany. On a wooded hill behind a Romanesque chapel, visitors walk along a path of statues representing Stations of the Cross or pray in an underground passage reminiscent of the Holy Sepulcher. A grotto to Our Lady of Lourdes is refreshed regularly with water from the original shrine in France.

The Shrine Chapel was built in 1910 from limestone quarried by parishioners. Plaques on the interior walls offer thanks (many in German) for answered prayers. A set of leg braces leans against a chapel altar, left there in 1935 by a young woman healed of polio. It's a place where sorrow gives way to hope.

A shrine built by a grateful town spared from a flood.

Crutches and a leg brace remain at the chapel of the Shrine of Our Lady of Sorrows after a young woman's prayers were answered.

Simeone issues a prophecy that Mary's soul will be pierced by a sword.
The Holy Family flees to Egypt to escape Herod.
Mary and Joseph lose Jesus in the Temple.
Mary encounters Jesus as He carries his cross to Calvary.
She witnesses the Crucifixion.
Her son's body is taken from the cross and laid in her arms.
Jesus is laid in the tomb.

The Seven Sorrows of Mary

A shrine to Ireland's patron saint.

Shrine of St. Patrick

St. Patrick

2 Erin Circle
St. Patrick 63466

Contact: post office next door
Stpatrickshrine.com

MAP LOCATION #7

The road to St. Patrick is narrow, winding among low hills past neatly kept farms and patches of woods. It's quiet and picturesque, and quite off the beaten path. You can't go much further north or east and still be in Missouri. The land was first settled in the 1830s by Irish immigrants. Their names are chiseled in the gravestones and Celtic crosses in the town's cemetery. As hard as life was on the Missouri frontier, it was far better than circumstances in Ireland, and the town grew around the church they built and named after their patron saint. Even though fewer than 20 people live in the town of St. Patrick today, its ethnic past is immediately obvious.

A painted statue of the saint himself stands beside the road in front of his shrine, which was dedicated in 1957 and modeled after St. Patrick's Memorial Church of the Four Masters in Donegal, Ireland. It was the idea of their parish priest, Fr. Francis O'Duignan from County Longford. Its round bell tower and Celtic crosses leave no doubt regarding its heritage.

Thirty-seven stained glass windows, created in Dublin, depict images of saints. A side altar to St. Patrick features the likenesses of St. Columbkille, St. Lawrence O'Toole, and St. Brigid.

There are more than a thousand churches in the world named after St. Patrick, but only one town. You are welcome to visit and pray there whenever you like, but March 17th would be most appropriate.

A touch of Ireland in rural Missouri.

St. George Catholic Church

Hermann

128 W 4th St.   573.486.2723   MAP LOCATION #8
Hermann 65041   Stghermann.diojeffcity.org

It's a long, steep climb up Fourth Street to St. George Church, but it's worth the effort. The views of downtown Hermann and the surrounding countryside are magnificent. Hermann is Missouri's quintessential German river town, a little piece of the Rhine Valley nestled among the bluffs and hills of the Missouri River. It's a place where important buildings like the county courthouse and the Catholic church reside upon hilltops.

The first St. George Church was a simple stone structure built in 1850. The present church replaced it in 1916, though the bell tower, a turn-of-the-century addition, was preserved. Statues of Franciscan saints serve as reminders of the many years Franciscan Friars of the Sacred Heart Province in St. Louis ran the church. Two artistically inclined brothers carved the altars from local butternut trees.

During the day the nave is bathed in soft light from stained glass windows created in Germany. Unlike most church windows, which represent scenes from Scripture, the windows of St. George depict the corporal and spiritual works of mercy.

Hermann is a town inspired by the Old World and an earlier time. It's impossible to imagine it without St. George Church, solid, confident, and German, perched in its high place on the hill, as close to Heaven as the local geography allows.

> Faithful servant of God and invincible martyr, St. George,
> favored by God with the gift of faith,
> and inflamed with an ardent love of Christ,
> thou didst fight valiantly
> against the dragon of pride, falsehood, and deceit.
> Neither pain nor torture, sword nor death
> could part thee from the love of Christ.
>
> Valiant champion of the Faith, assist me in the combat against evil,
> that I may win the crown promised to them that persevere unto the end.
>
> *From St. George Novena*

Easter decorations in St. Joseph's corner of St. George Church.

St. Cecilia, patron saint of music, stands beside the altar of St. Louis of France.

St. Louis of France Catholic Church

Bonnots Mill

211 Church Hill St.   573.897.2922   **MAP LOCATION #9**
Bonnots Mill 65016

In a region known for its Germanic roots, Bonnots Mill stands apart. A group of French Canadians built the town in the 1850s on a bluff overlooking the confluence of the Osage and Missouri rivers. For decades it thrived as a riverboat and railroad town. At the foot of the bluff, its tiny downtown is a piece of Midwest Americana. Church Hill Street is a steep climb up the hill to the St. Louis of France Catholic Church. Beyond the church at the top of the bluff is a view of the rivers that has changed little since the town's early days.

Catholics attended churches in surrounding towns until St. Louis of France opened in 1906. At the time, the area around Jefferson City was still within the Archdiocese of St. Louis, and Archbishop John Glennon, who thought it was time for the town to have a Catholic church, bought three acres on the bluff for six dollars.

The parish built a church that is a testament to modesty, a small, wood frame structure without a trace of pretension. Its lack of Old World embellishments lends it an air of simple honesty and quiet confidence. It invites visitors to a place of humility.

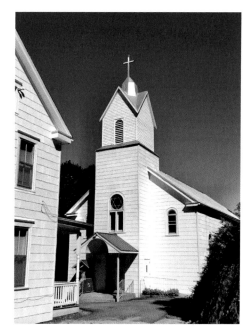

Rectory and church
of St. Louis of France.

Novenas

A novena (from *novem*, Latin for "nine") is a series of prayers, offered every day for nine consecutive days. The number nine has long been considered significant among many cultures. The Greeks and Romans held nine-day periods of mourning after funerals. The first Christian novena is said to be the nine days between Jesus's Ascension and Pentecost, during which the Apostles, Mary, and a group of disciples prayed for guidance from the Holy Spirit. In the Middle Ages, novenas became a widespread ritual to petition for favors.

What makes novenas special is that they require some commitment and preparation. First, you need to decide what you're praying for, then choose a particular novena, schedule a block of time, and then actually say the prayers. There are hundreds of novenas. Some are traditional; others have identifiable authors, including some saints. Some are said upon special occasions, like a feast day, holiday, or wedding. Novenas are said for those who die and those who mourn them. Some novenas are offered for penance, and sometimes they are intercessions for ourselves or someone close to us. Novenas can be offered to saints, angels, persons of the Trinity, and various manifestations of the Holy Mother.

People pray novenas for different reasons. We tend to place more value on efforts that require some self-discipline. Novenas impose some structure in a world where our prayers often take a backseat to the distractions and requirements of daily life. Dedication to a novena keeps us grounded, at least for nine days. Praying for the intercession of a saint or holy figure allows us to personalize our prayers and make them more suitable to our purpose. When we pray a novena with friends, family, or fellow parishioners, we receive the strength of a larger community. We feel less alone.

But novenas are not magic spells or incantations, and there is no guarantee that they will be answered in the way you hope or expect. You might not get what you ask, but there's a good chance you'll get what you need. Be patient. God's world is bigger than ours. You might recognize the answer to your prayer at a different time and in a different way than you expected. When that happens, it's hard not to smile. It's how the Holy Spirit works.

Votive candles at St. Anthony of Padua Catholic Church, St. Louis.

A shrine to Our Lady of Sorrows beside St. Paul Catholic Church.

St. Paul Catholic Church

Center

St. Paul Dr.
Center 63436

MAP LOCATION #10

Known as the mother church of Roman Catholicism in northeast Missouri, St. Paul Church today is more of a historic site and museum than an active church. That it's still standing is a tribute to the resilience of its supporters in a rural, generally non-Catholic part of the state.

The first Catholics came to the region from Virginia and Kentucky after the War of 1812, but their small numbers and scattered farms made it difficult to attract full-time priests to their humble log church. In 1860, parishioners built the church that stands today at the end of a narrow lane a few miles outside Center, Missouri.

The church has been closed since 1966, but it is well-maintained by a loyal group that raises funds through an annual barbecue and ice cream social. There are occasional tours and even a Mass from time to time. Funerals are still conducted in the adjoining cemetery, where three veterans of the American Revolution are buried. A shrine to Our Lady of Sorrows stands beneath a canopy of trees, and a walkway leads visitors through a wooded area where seven statues depict the Sorrows of the Holy Mother.

A visit to St. Paul Church is a trip back to a time when people packed their faith along with a few possessions to leave their homes and search for a better life in a foreign world. When you visit, it's very possible that you will be the only person there. If you are quiet, you might sense the spirit of those who worshipped here, and when you touch the stones of the old church or walk through the graveyard, you will participate in the history of their faith.

Mother church of Catholic northeast Missouri.

St. Peter Catholic Church

(Brush Creek Church)

Brush Creek

14690 Gentry Rd.
Monroe City 63456

MAP LOCATION #11

St. Peter Church is a humble country church at the end of a tree-lined lane in a rural stretch of northeast Missouri. A small corner of its cemetery is the resting place for the enslaved people who once lived nearby. Many of its small white crosses are broken. Some have the word "Unknown" written upon them.

The old church has stood there since 1862, when it replaced an even simpler log building. It closed in 1967, and today Masses are only occasionally held there. Some visitors come to appreciate the peaceful, rural setting and the historical architecture. Others make the trip to honor the site where the nation's first African American Catholic priest was baptized.

Many of the first Catholics to settle in the area were southern slaveowners. Augustus Tolton, the son of an enslaved couple, was baptized at St. Peter in 1854. When the Civil War came to the region, Augustus and his parents escaped to Quincy, Illinois. Augustus was called to the priesthood but couldn't find an American seminary that

would accept a Black applicant. He traveled to Rome and was ordained there in 1886.

Fr. Tolton returned to the United States, where he led the founding of St. Monica's Catholic Church in Chicago, the nation's first parish built and operated by African Americans. His cause of canonization was opened in 2010 and he was declared Venerable by Pope Francis in 2019.

Fr. Augustus Tolton (1854–1897).

The main altar of St. Peter in Jefferson City presents a statue of the Sacred Heart of Jesus, accompanied by Saints Peter and Paul.

St. Peter Catholic Church

Jefferson City

216 Broadway St.
Jefferson City 65101

573.636.8159
Saintpeterjc.org

MAP LOCATION #12

In 1838, Jefferson City's nine Catholic families began gathering in each other's homes to celebrate Mass. As Jesuit missionaries and immigrants from Germany, Italy, and Ireland pushed west, parishes grew in Jefferson City and nearby towns. The current St. Peter opened in 1883, 34 years before today's Capitol building opened for business just outside its front door.

It was a structure whose grandeur made it clear that Catholicism had arrived in central Missouri. A gothic masterpiece, it was designed by Adolphus Druiding, the architect for such grand St. Louis churches as St. John Nepomuk, St. Agatha, St. Alphonsus Liguori, and the Shrine of St. Joseph.

St. Peter is a source of pride for the entire community, regardless of faith. It's a sanctuary from the world of government and politics that surrounds it. By all appearances, church and state seem to reside comfortably together there in the heart of town, each attending to its own concerns.

According to tradition, the swearing-in of the governor begins after the bell in St. Peter Church strikes the noon Angelus on Inauguration Day.

St. Stephen Catholic Church

Indian Creek

27519 Monroe Co. Rd. 533   573.735.4718
Indian Creek 63456   Ststephenic.diojeffcity.org

MAP LOCATION #13

Before it was Indian Creek, it was Elizabethtown. And Swinkey. Because a town that's been around for almost 200 years is bound to go through lots of changes. St. Stephen parish has seen it all, rolled with the punches, and stands today as a symbol of a town's faith in God and itself.

Many of the first townsfolk were Irish immigrants. In the early days the town was a trading center, post office, and gathering spot for weekend horse races. St. Stephen's opened in 1833, which makes it the oldest parish in the Jefferson City Diocese. The first two churches burned down. The third was destroyed in 1876, when a cyclone flattened most of the town. According to local legend, the sanctuary lamp was still burning when rescuers found it on a pile of rubble near the altar.

God continued to test the resolve of Indian Creek's faithful. A new church rose from the old foundation. But when lightning struck its steeple in 1907, the ensuing fire left it badly damaged. By that time the parishioners of St. Stephen had grown skilled at rebuilding, and later that year the church that stands there today was dedicated, though with a shorter steeple.

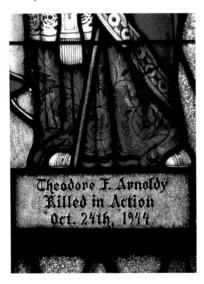

St. Stephen is the heart of a small, close community with a long and shared history. Families of the original settlers still attend Mass there. On both sides of the altar, stained glass windows memorialize the death of a young parishioner, killed in World War II. This town and its church have earned their place on the banks of Indian Creek.

An epitaph in stained glass.

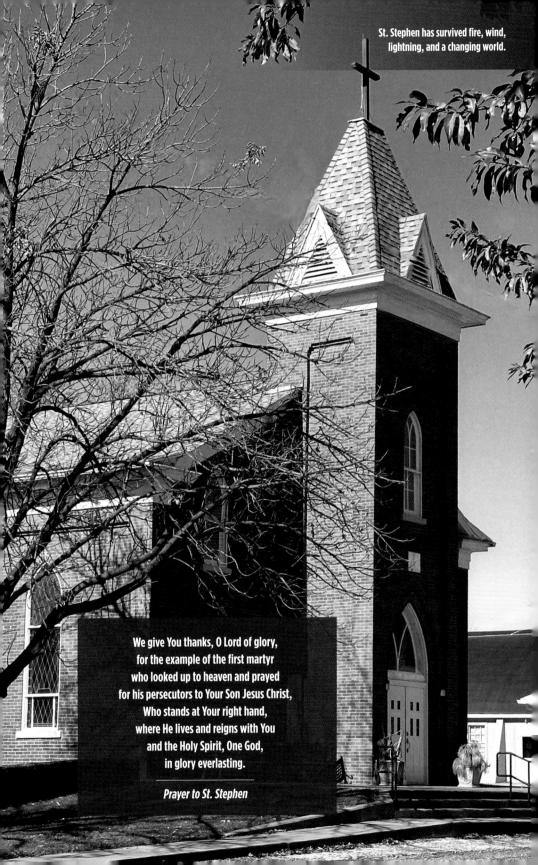

St. Stephen has survived fire, wind, lightning, and a changing world.

We give You thanks, O Lord of glory,
for the example of the first martyr
who looked up to heaven and prayed
for his persecutors to Your Son Jesus Christ,
Who stands at Your right hand,
where He lives and reigns with You
and the Holy Spirit, One God,
in glory everlasting.

Prayer to St. Stephen

Lectio Divina

(Divine Reading)

Words that endure for thousands of years need to be taken seriously, particularly when the purpose of those words is to help us understand God. It's unfortunate that so many of us feel unworthy of fully understanding them without a degree in theology. If only there were a way to approach Holy Scripture in a way that releases its wonder and joy so that we might be touched personally.

Enter *Lectio Divina* (Latin for Divine Reading). It's a formula for reading Scripture that was developed and refined by monks between the sixth and twelfth centuries. Its popularity has spread steadily since the Second Vatican Council recommended it as a practice for everyone.

Lectio Divina is a four-step approach toward Scripture that treats it not as some ponderous puzzle to analyze, but as a living source of inspiration. It's a process that employs imagination and intuition while relying on the Holy Spirit for guidance.

The first step is to put yourself in an undistracted state of mind and then slowly and thoughtfully read, maybe more than once, a passage of Scripture that interests you. Focus on words and phrases that resonate with you.

Next, meditate on the passage, opening yourself to the possibility of illumination from the Holy Spirit. Put yourself inside the text as if it were a scene from life, and you were there. Visualize the details. Imagine and explore how the words apply to your most personal thoughts, hopes, and history.

Pray. Engage in a loving conversation with God based upon your insights. Remember, it's a conversation. God might have something to say. You wouldn't want to miss that.

Finally, take some time for contemplation. Just be quiet for a while and rest in God's presence. Receive. Silence is a good place for a soul to find union with God. This could be the time when you discover new patterns of behavior you might want to apply to your daily life.

If you find *Lectio Divina* a useful tool, be glad that there's no shortage of Scripture and no limits to the new horizons that may reveal themselves to you.

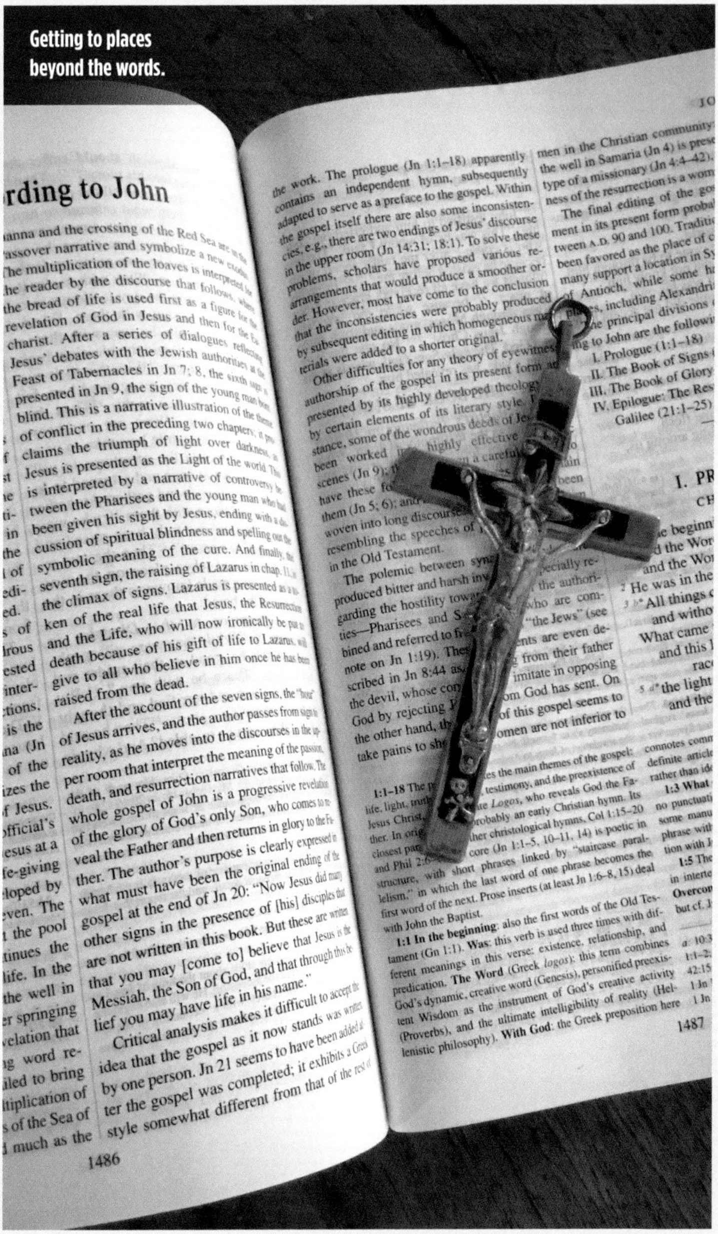
Getting to places
beyond the words.
rding to John
1486
1487

MISSISSIPPI
RIVER

HWY 55

RT 61

RT 177

RT 51

CAPE GIRARDEAU

RT 34

2 3

CAPE GIRARDEAU   RT 146

RT 3

RT 65

RT 25

6

HWY 44

RT 13

NEW HAMBURG

RT 13

5

HWY 44

SPRINGFIELD

RT 60

HWY 55

RT 160

RT 61

RT 77

RT 14

SPRINGFIELD

RT 65

1

AVA

RT 5

4

BRANSON

RT 160

SEE CORRESPONDING NUMBERS
ON THE FOLLOWING PAGES.

TABLE ROCK LAKE

RT 412

BULL SHOALS LAKE

Diocese of Springfield–Cape Girardeau

Assumption Abbey

Ava

R. R. 5, Box 1056   417.683.5110   **MAP LOCATION #1**
Ava 65608   Assumptionabbey.org

The Abbey's address appears as Ava, Missouri, but from the main intersection of that tiny town, it's at least a half-hour drive through the Ozarks to Assumption Abbey. That's remote.

Assumption has been home to a community of Trappist monks since 1950. Their first quarters were an old, donated house without running water or electricity. For years they sustained themselves by raising sheep, planting orchards, and producing wine. The rocky soil eventually ended their agricultural aspirations, and they began dredging the creeks for gravel and making concrete blocks. That enterprise grew successful enough to finance construction of their current monastery.

In the late 1980s, the monks inherited a commercial oven from a St. Louis supermarket and made the unlikely switch from concrete blocks to fruitcakes. Today they support themselves by selling their own brand of self-made fruitcakes to thousands of loyal customers throughout the world.

Trappist monks follow the Rule of St. Benedict, a strict regimen of contemplation, prayer, and work. Though not sworn to silence, they tend to speak only when necessary. Benedictine tradition calls for treating guests, regardless of their faith, as if they are Christ, so hospitality is a prime virtue, and a comfortable guesthouse is reserved for visitors. Guests are welcome to dine and pray with the monks or schedule their personal time however they wish. The grounds offer 3,000 acres of heavily wooded hills to explore. For the less physically ambitious, there's a comfortable and well-stocked library.

Over the years the monastery has gone through other changes. As the first generation of American-born monks aged and passed away, their places were filled by monks from a monastery in central Vietnam. Today most of the monks at Assumption are Vietnamese.

The remote location, cultural diversity, and possibly the best fruitcake you have ever eaten will certainly set your retreat at Assumption Abbey apart from any other you are likely to experience.

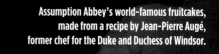

Assumption Abbey's world-famous fruitcakes, made from a recipe by Jean-Pierre Augé, former chef for the Duke and Duchess of Windsor.

Cistercian Monks

Assumption Abbey Fruitcake

BAKED BY THE MONKS OF ASSUMPTION ABBEY

IMPORTANT SERVING SUGGESTIONS

To serve your fruitcake at its finest we suggest that you first chill it. Using a sharp knife, slice with even sawing motions. Wiping the blade with a wet cloth after each slice also helps. Bring to room temperature before serving.

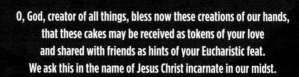

O, God, creator of all things, bless now these creations of our hands,
that these cakes may be received as tokens of your love
and shared with friends as hints of your Eucharistic feat.
We ask this in the name of Jesus Christ incarnate in our midst.

Daily blessing of the fruitcakes

Mary stands beside the door
of her cathedral in Cape Girardeau.

Cathedral of St. Mary of the Annunciation

Cape Girardeau

615 William St.
Cape Girardeau 63703

573.335.9347
Stmarycathedral.net

MAP LOCATION #2

The Diocese of Springfield-Cape Girardeau encompasses the lower third of the state with a cathedral at each end: St. Agnes in Springfield and St. Mary of the Annunciation in Cape Girardeau. Catholics in the diocese tend to be more spread out than in other parts of the state.

For years German Catholics in Cape Girardeau worshipped at St. Vincent's downtown. St. Mary opened in 1869 to fulfill their hopes for a church of their own. The interior is carefully decorated. Stained glass windows portray *The Magnificat*. *The Annunciation*, originally painted by Spanish Baroque artist Bartolomé Esteban Murillo, fills a space behind the altar of this cathedral that honors the Mother of God.

Copy of Murillo's *The Annunciation* is a local treasure.

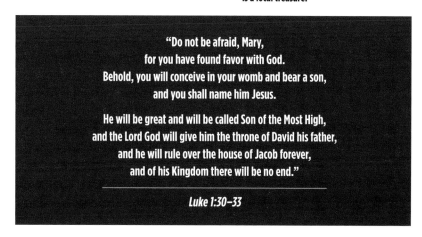

"Do not be afraid, Mary,
for you have found favor with God.
Behold, you will conceive in your womb and bear a son,
and you shall name him Jesus.

He will be great and will be called Son of the Most High,
and the Lord God will give him the throne of David his father,
and he will rule over the house of Jacob forever,
and of his Kingdom there will be no end."

Luke 1:30–33

Veneration of Mary and the Saints

This is where a lot of non-Catholics draw the line. Praying to anybody who's not a part of the Holy Trinity smacks of idolatry, and that's bad enough to be forbidden by the very first commandment. So the objection is understandable. But there's a difference between worshipping and venerating, and that's the source of the confusion. Veneration is respect. Worship is a much higher level of respect, reserved only for God. Prayer is a petition or entreaty, and prayers to Mary or the saints are essentially requests to put in a good word for us to God. It's not that different from asking a friend to pray for us. Statues of Mary in a grotto or Mass cards of St. Patrick on the refrigerator aren't graven images or false idols; they are treasured reminders, like family photos.

Mary doesn't say much in the Gospels, but when she does, her words are always full of good sense and wisdom. Maybe like your own mom. Other saints offer us comfort because they overcame flaws much like our own. St. Peter made bad decisions. St. Augustine enjoyed enough good times as a young man to write a best-seller of Confessions. St. Dismas was a thief. Others inspire us with their grace. The holy goofiness of St. Francis is irresistible. We have much to learn from St. Joseph's patient willingness to set his ego aside. The gentle serenity of St. Thérèse of Lisieux calls out for us to smell the roses and follow her on her Little Way.

What harm could there be in asking these wonderful human beings to help us through our time on earth and share with us their closeness to God?

Mary in a window of
St. Agnes Cathedral in Springfield.

My soul proclaims the greatness of the Lord,
my spirit rejoices in God my Savior,
for he has looked with favor on his lowly servant.
From this day all generations will call me blessed:
the Almighty has done great things for me,
and holy is his Name.
He has mercy on those who fear him
in every generation.
He has shown the strength of his arm,
he has scattered the proud in their conceit.
He has cast down the mighty from their thrones,
and has lifted up the lowly.
He has filled the hungry with good things,
and the rich he has sent away empty.
He has come to the help of his servant Israel
for he has remembered his promise of mercy,
the promise he made to our fathers,
to Abraham and his children forever.

The Magnificat

Old St. Vincent's Catholic Church

Cape Girardeau

131 S Main St.
Cape Girardeau 63703

573.651.3433
Oldstvincents.org

MAP LOCATION #3

If not for the efforts of a few dedicated souls, this architectural masterpiece would have been torn down in the 1970s. Renowned Irish architect Thomas Waryng Walsh designed it in the style of English Gothic, which is extraordinarily rare. Today Old St. Vincent's is designated a "chapel of ease," meaning that even though it's no longer a parish, it's still open for worship.

Spared from the wrecking ball, the church underwent a major renovation. Liturgical architects and interior designers consulted archival records to bring the interior of the church to its original condition. The result is impressive. Gothic arches lend it grace and delicacy. The altars, pews, and wrought-iron communion rail are original. More than a hundred plaster masks representing figures from medieval mystery plays peek out at the congregation. Rows of elegant columns rise beneath wooden beams supporting the roof.

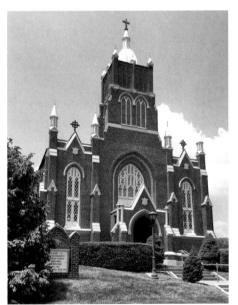

The atmosphere is that of a 15th-century English church.

Old St. Vincent's stands as a memorial to the devotion of its original parishioners and to their descendants, who appreciated what they had inherited and worked to keep it alive.

Occupying a prominent place on the city's Mississippi riverfront since 1853.

Christmas at Old St. Vincent's.
Photo, Old St. Vincent Archives.

A statue of Our Lady of Guadalupe attests to Our Lady of the Lake's growing Hispanic membership. *Photo, Our Lady of the Lake.*

Our Lady of the Lake Catholic Church

Branson

203 Vaughn Rd.   417.334.2928   **MAP LOCATION #4**
Branson 65616   Ollbranson.com

Located in the heart of the Bible Belt, Branson's Catholics have always been a small but close-knit community. Today fewer than five percent of the town's residents are Catholic, and Our Lady of the Lake is their only church. For years it was a small church in a small town, until Branson's amazing transformation into a major entertainment center turned the church into a destination for Catholic tourists from around the world.

The area around Branson became famous as a vacation paradise in 1907 after publication of Harold Bell Wright's bestseller, *The Shepherd of the Hills*. As curious readers drifted in to see the real-life setting for the book, local entrepreneurs saw opportunities to develop local attractions, which evolved into bigger enterprises like Marvel Cave and Silver Dollar City. The creation of Table Rock Lake in 1959 brought more tourists looking for places to spend their money. By the 1980s, the town's theaters were featuring the hottest entertainment acts in the country. In 1991, CBS's *60 Minutes* proclaimed Branson the "live music capital of the entire universe."

It's not the typical story of a Catholic church in the Ozarks. In 1936, Our Lady of the Lake celebrated Mass in an abandoned bank. Today it serves more than 500 families, celebrating Mass in both Spanish and English. A tourist boom lasting decades was hardly inevitable. But it happened. And as a small town pursued its dreams of success in the world of show business, its small, Catholic community created a spiritual home that opens its doors to a steady stream of worshippers from every part of the globe.

St. Agnes Roman Catholic Cathedral

Springfield

533 S Jefferson Ave. 417.831.3565 **MAP LOCATION #5**
Springfield 65806 Sta-cathedral.org

The story of Catholicism in Missouri is mostly about European immigrants creating places for themselves in city neighborhoods and small towns. The bigger picture is different. Most of the early settlers were native-born Americans from Kentucky, Tennessee, and Virginia. Many of them were Protestant, descendants of the English and Scots Irish, and often hostile to Catholic newcomers. Much of southern Missouri today is Evangelical Christian, and Springfield is often called the "Buckle of the Bible Belt."

Springfield's first Catholic parish, Immaculate Conception, was established in 1866. When the Atlantic and Pacific Railroad came through town in 1870, large numbers of German and Irish Catholics moved into the city. But as more families settled into neighborhoods on both sides of the tracks, the railroad became a physical barrier dividing the town's Catholics. Many were reluctant to make the trip across town to attend Mass, calling the tracks "a menace to life and limb." In 1908, the diocese formed a second parish on the far side of the tracks and two years later built St. Agnes.

The church's interior is contemporary with a simple elegance. In a mural above the altar, Christ raises his hands above the individual churches of the diocese. Rows of stained glass windows along the walls of the nave are remnants of the original construction, illuminating the interior in soft, colored light.

When the Diocese of Springfield-Cape Girardeau was created in 1956, two diocesan cathedrals were chosen, one at each end of the state. Springfield's St. Agnes was elevated to the rank of cathedral. St. Mary of the Annunciation in Cape Girardeau became the diocese's co-cathedral.

From the altar of St. Agnes, Christ blesses the churches of the diocese.

Visio Divina

(Divine Seeing)

There are many ways to pray, because we all express ourselves differently. We share the same senses but respond to them in varying degrees. Some of us are particularly sensitive to sounds and easily touched by the power of music. Others find their imaginations enlivened by the written word. Many of us are affected by the shapes, colors, and forms of visual images. Long before there were cognitive psychologists, the Catholic Church understood these differences and encouraged pathways to prayer that lead us through our own personal landscapes of imagination, where all things are possible.

Visio Divina is a lot like *Lectio Divina*, except it directs our focus of prayer to visual images rather than passages of Scripture. It lets God speak to our hearts through works of art. This isn't new. For centuries, the Church has inspired our faith through the beauty of stained glass, architectural design, icons, statues, and more.

The process isn't difficult. First, you'll want to choose an image. That could be as simple as checking out an art book from the library. It can have a religious theme, but it could also be a piece of contemporary or abstract art. If you're feeling adventurous, you might pick out a comfortable spot with a view in a local park or a nearby forest. The point is to have something visual to focus on.

Ask God to speak to you through the image. Clear your mind, then truly look at it. Take it all in, close your eyes for a moment, then study it again. Submerge yourself, as if you are a part of it. Ask yourself, what thoughts or feelings come to mind? If you were in the picture, where would you be, and what would you be doing? Listen. Could this exercise possibly be a conversation with God? If you're not sure what to expect or what you experienced, try it again.

If Creation itself comes from the Imagination of God, it's reasonable to think that our own, small imaginations might be pathways to the Divine. Imagination, given by God and inspired by art, allows us passage into the realms of saints and angels, where miracles are possible and prayers are heard.

The St. John's Bible is an extraordinary presentation of Scripture accompanied by visual interpretations.

Elisha and the Six Miracles, Donald Jackson with contributions from Aidan Hart, Copyright 2010, *The Saint John's Bible*, Saint John's University, Minnesota USA. Used with permission. All rights reserved.

St. Lawrence Catholic Church

New Hamburg

1017 State Hwy. A　　　573.545.3317　　　**MAP LOCATION #6**
New Hamburg 63736

The steeple of St. Lawrence is visible on the horizon long before there's any sign of a town. New Hamburg is a half-hour drive south of Cape Girardeau through landscapes that haven't changed much since the first German settlers arrived there from Alsace-Lorraine. The original log church from 1847 has been restored and stands on the grounds at the edge of the old parish cemetery.

Work began in 1858 on a larger stone church on a hill in the center of town. A local schoolteacher designed the plan, relying on his memory of St. Nicolas Church in his hometown of Schirrhein on the French-German border. Parishioners were asked to either pay five dollars, deliver eight wagonloads of stones, or work every tenth day at the construction site. The church was almost completed when Southern troops burned it down during the Civil War. Only the walls remained,

and the parish rebuilt it in 1869. After the war, surrounding communities built their own churches.

Today St. Lawrence is considered the mother church of the region.

St. Lawrence was rebuilt by its parishioners after being burned by Confederate troops.

Roman martyr St. Lawrence keeps his place at the main altar of the church that bears his name.

St. PAUL

More Places to Pray

Living Insights/Clayton
Livinginsights.com

Displaying religious artifacts from world religions, this small house is more a museum than a church, but its distinctly sacred atmosphere is undeniable. A statue of St. Thérèse de Lisieux is believed by many to have healing powers.

St. Ann Catholic Church/Clover Bottom
Stannchurchcloverbottom.org

Legend has it that when Polish immigrants built St. Ann from locally hewn stone, the surrounding fields were filled with clover. Today its simple elegance retains a flavor of Eastern European culture.

St. John the Baptist—Gildehaus Catholic Church/Villa Ridge
Sjg-parish.org

Tucked into a quiet place among gently rolling hills, nothing suggests a troubled past. But during the Civil War, Federal troops burned the original log church. When parishioners rebuilt it, they inserted a beam from the ruins beneath the loft. Inscribed upon it are the words "The House of God, the Gate of Heaven."

St. Vincent De Paul/Dutzow

Perched atop a river bluff and surrounded by an old graveyard, St. Vincent is a charming 1870s church located in the heart of wine country. Dutzow also has the distinction of being a stop on the Katy bike trail and the former home of Gottfried Duden, who in the 1830s popularized Missouri as a destination for German immigrants.

Shrine to the Holy Family/Foristell
Cedarlakefoundation.org

Surrounded by fields and forest, a small pavilion beside a pond shelters a sculpture of the Holy Family in a playful moment. It's perfect for family outings, a place for picnics and prayer while the kids chase the ducks.

More Places to Pray

Precious Blood Renewal Center/Liberty
Pbrenewalcenter.org

Open to all faiths, Precious Blood is a place where visitors are encouraged through a variety of programs to find peace and forgiveness in a beautiful, natural setting. The grounds include trails, a small lake, and a labyrinth, where they are free to meditate and open themselves to God's plan.

Shrine to Our Lady of Guadalupe/Kansas City
Sacredheartguadalupe.org

For over a century, this small, stone church has been a vital center for Kansas City's Mexican community. A large sculpture outside its door portrays Juan Diego on his knees before Our Lady as she appears to him in a vision.

Sacred Heart Catholic Church/Rich Fountain
Sacredheartrf.com

Built by Bavarian Catholics, Sacred Heart is known for the fine work of its craftsmen. Built on a rocky ridge from limestone blocks, it has a look of grace and permanence. White altars are set against a red sanctuary, and paintings depict Christ the King flanked by angels. Lest there be any doubts as to who made this, the Stations of the Cross bear captions written in German.

St. Stanislaus Catholic Church/Wardsville
Ststanislaus.net

St. Stanislaus is one of many churches built by German immigrants in small towns clustered around Jefferson City. It is small but stately with a distinctly Old World atmosphere. Soft light from stained glass windows bathes an interior of limestone and dark wood containing a rich collection of liturgical art.

Congregation of the Mother of the Redeemer (Marian Days)/Carthage

Located in the heart of Evangelical Protestant southern Missouri, this Vietnamese congregation has sponsored Marian Days every August since 1978. The four-day festival attracts thousands of visitors to a celebration of Vietnamese culture and devotion to the Virgin Mary.

Sunrise in Pacific, Missouri.

i thank You God for most this amazing day;
for leaping greenly spirits of trees and a blue true dream of sky;
and for everything which is natural which is infinite which is yes.

E. E. Cummings

Afterword

As you make your pilgrimages to holy sites throughout the state, look for opportunities to get off the highways. It's no time to be in a hurry, and Missouri's back roads pass through some of the most beautiful countryside in America. If you're at all inclined to offer prayers of gratitude, you will find inspiration at every bend in the road.

Connecting with God by being present in the created world is as much a prayer as any you may offer at a shrine, a church, or a grotto. Nature has the power to calm our minds and let us see God in the patterns of bare branches against a winter sunset or the way a summer breeze ripples a sea of grasslands beneath a giant sky.

You may get a brief sense of the immensity of God's Time from the top of an ancient Ozarks mountain or a bluff carved by one of Missouri's great rivers. You might be awed by the infinitely overlapping network of life as bees and butterflies chase the flowers from spring to autumn and birds fill the woods with songs only they understand.

Creation surpasses the beauty of any church we could build to honor God, and if being truly present in the midst of it all makes you feel small, take comfort that it is a gift. You are free to express your thanks with words or silence.

Sources

Abeln, Mark S. "Photos of Saint George Catholic Church in Hermann, Missouri." Rome of the West. November 18, 2006. Romeofthewest.com.

Agatha, Sr. Mary, CMRI. "Our Mother of Perpetual Help, History of the Miraculous Icon." The Religious Congregation of Mary Immaculate Queen. https://cmri.org/articles-on-the-traditional-catholic-faith/our-mother-of-perpetual-help/.

Aschenbrenner, George. "Consciousness Examen." https://www.ignatianspirituality.com/ignatian-prayer/the-examen/consciousness-examen/.

Beck, Jo. "LaSalle Institute Remains Historic District." 2011. https://patch.com/missouri/eureka-wildwood/la-salle-institute-remains-historic-landmark.

Brinker, Jennifer. "Practices of Lectio Divina, *Visio Divina* Allow Us to More Fully Immerse Ourselves Into Scripture."
St. Louis Review, October 4–10, 2021.

"Built St. Louis. MidCentury Modernism. The Emil Frei Stained Glass Company." https://www.builtstlouis.net/mod/emil-frei-stained-glass.html.

Burnett, Robyn, and Luebbering, Ken. *German Settlement in Missouri*. University of Missouri Press. Columbia. 1996.

Cernich, Karen. "A Lot of History, A Lot of Faith—Borgia to Celebrate 150th Anniversary of Third Church." *The Missourian*. May 31, 2019.

"Chapel of the Precious Blood." Discalced Carmelite Nuns. https://www.stlouiscarmel.com/legion-of-one-thousand-west/worship/.

Clough, Daniel. *The History of St Mary of Victories Church*. St. Louis. 2007.

Coleman, Michael, Fr., Beemont, Bill R., Marra, Dorothy Brandt, Doering, Colette. *This Far by Faith*. Walsworth Publishing Co. 1992.

Coons, Cami. "Lady of Guadalupe Consolidation." March 28, 2022. https://flatlandkc.org/curiouskc/curiouskc-remembering-the-sacred-heart-and-our-lady-of-guadalupe-consolidation/.

Cooperman, Jeannette. "Inside the Enclosure," *St. Louis Magazine*, July 28, 2006.

Daugherty, Zachary S. *Images of America: Catholic Kansas City*. Arcadia Publishing. Charleston, South Carolina. 2021.

Denny, James M. "The Irish Wilderness: The Curious History of an Ozarks Place." *Ozarks Watch*, Vol. V, No. 3, Winter 1992.

Denzer, Marty. "Historic Parish a Place to Come Home To." *Catholic Key*. Kansas City. December 6, 2019.

Duricy, Michael. "All About Mary. Black Madonnas: Origin, History, Controversy." https://udayton.edu/imri/mary/b/black-madonnas-origin-history-controversy.php/.

Faherty, Barnaby, SJ. *Catholic St. Louis: A Pictorial History*. Reedy Press. St. Louis. 2009.

Franey, Tom, and Junge, Marian. *Sharing the Mission: 150 Years of Service to St. Louis by the Parish of St. Vincent de Paul*.

Gaultiere, Bill. "Discover The Power of Ignatian Meditation to Engage with Jesus." https://www.soulshepherding.org/ignatian-meditation-guides/.

Glines, Karen, and O'Donnell, Billyo. *Painting Missouri*. University of Missouri Press. Columbia. 2008.

Hahn, Valerie Schremp. "A Saint's Footsteps, A Monk's Handiwork, A Miraculous Medal." *St. Louis Today*, April 5, 2021.

Harris, NiNi. *Bohemian Hill: An American Story*. St. John Nepomuk Parish. St. Louis. 2004.

Harris, NiNi. *Saint Gabriel the Archangel*. Reedy Press. St. Louis. 2009.

"History of the Carmel of St. Joseph." Discalced Carmelite Nuns. https://www.stlouiscarmel.com/history-of-the-carmel-of-st-joseph/.

Mangan, Rev. Charles. "Church Teaching on Relics." *Arlington Catholic Herald*. 2003. https://catholiceducation.org/en/culture/catholic-contributions/church-teaching-on-relics.html.

Naffziger, Chris. "Interior, Most Holy Trinity Roman Catholic Church." Stlouispatina.com. April 25, 2022.

Naffziger, Chris. "St. Agatha's Catholic Church, Revisited." Stlouispatina.com. July 19, 2020.

Naffziger, Chris. "St. James the Greater Catholic Church." Stlouispatina.com. December 23, 2020.

Nies, Jay. "175 Years and Counting for St. Joseph in Edina." The *Catholic Missourian*. Jefferson City. December 19, 2019.

Nies, Jay. "Renovated Cathedral Will Showcase Beauty of Our Catholic Faith." The *Catholic Missourian*. Jefferson City. March 4, 2022.

O'Connor, Rev. P.J. "History of Cheltenham and St. James Parish." St. Louis. 1937.

Pastava, Loretta, SND. "The Catholic Church in Southern Missouri." Editions du Signe. Strassbourg. 2005.

Petkova, Martina. "The Mystery of the Black Madonna." August 6, 2020. https://historyofyesterday.com/the-mystery-of-the-black-madonna-a0503c51537/.

Royackers, Fr. Martin, SJ, ed. "A Method of Making the General Examen." From "The Spiritual Exercises of St. Ignatius Loyola." July 2, 2019. https://manresa-canada.ca/blog/2019/02/02/a-method-of-making-the-general-examen/.

Shirey, Kathryn. "*Visio Divina*: How to Pray with the 'Eyes of Your Heart.'" February 4, 2019. https://www.prayerandpossibiliites.com/pray-with-eyes-of-the-heart-visio-divina/.

Silvey, Jennifer. "A Timeline of Irish History in Kansas City to Celebrate St. Patrick's Day." Fox 4. Kansas City. March 17, 2019. Fox4kc.com.

Snider, Felix Eugene & Collins, Earl Augustus. *Cape Girardeau Biography of a City*. Ramfre Press. Cape Girardeau. 1956.

Sonnen, John Paul. "The Abbey of Our Lady of Ephesus." *Liturgical Arts Journal*. May 21, 2021.

Stiles, Nancy. "Sequestered in the Missouri Ozarks, These Monks Made 30,000 Fruitcakes a Year." *Feast Magazine*. 2017.

Works Progress Administration. *Missouri: A Guide to the "Show Me" State*. Hastings House Publishers. New York. 1954.

Index